Loose Sandhills:

The Story of Salishan

Loose Sandhills

The Story of Salishan

Mike Stone

INFINITY PUBLISHING

Copyright © 2006 by Mike Stone

ISBN 0-7414-3483-0

Published by:

INFINITY
PUBLISHING.COM

1094 New DeHaven Street, Suite 100
West Conshohocken, PA 19428-2713
Info"buybooksontheweb.com
www.buybooksontheweb.com
Toll-free (877) BUY BOOK
Local Phone (610) 941-9999
Fax (610) 941-9959

Printed in the United States of America

Printed on Recycled Paper

Published August 2006

CONTENTS

Dedicated to my wife
Susan Louise Stone

August 2006

Publication of this book would not have been possible without the assistance of numerous people.

A sincere thank you to John Gray for his indulgence during several interviews. As noted in this book, Mr. Gray is uncomfortable with publicity, preferring his lifetime of achievements tell his story.

Interviews with William Wyse, Gwen Stone, Robert Eaton, Donn DeBernardi, Phil Devito and Dave Pugh are particularly appreciated.

Attorney Phillip Schuster provided invaluable comments on early manuscripts.

Tom Brosy shared his collection of Salishan memories. Salishan residential manager Tom Trunt was always accommodating.

Thank you one and all!

Mike Stone

INTRODUCTION

"It was an opportunity for all of us to do our best"

Barbara Fealy

They made an unlikely business alliance; the quiet, unassuming Portland multi-millionaire and a major philanthropic force in Oregon; the iconoclastic, acerbic Portland architect; and the Portland female landscape architect with fierce independence and gentle creativity.

They merged their talents in the 1960s at a former Oregon coast dairy farm 95 miles southwest of Portland. The three would collaborate on a land development on a sand spit and a resort unlike any other in the Pacific Northwest, one which hosted governors, movie stars, and generations of Pacific Northwest families.

The resort would be called Salishan Lodge, a melding of native woods and shrubs, a tribute to Northwest artists, an understated elegance, and the defining tribute to the Portlanders; John and Betty Gray, John Storrs, and Barbara Fealy. Gray would later develop other resorts and properties such as Sunriver, Skamania Lodge, Johns Landing, and was the first developer to recognize the potential of Portland's Pearl District. Storrs would design more architectural masterpieces such as the World Forestry Center; and Fealy would apply her landscape genius to other Oregon lands including Timberline Lodge. But it was Salishan Lodge that would always be highlighted in their biographical sketches, the Salishan Lodge which stood out among many mundane and architecturally drab Oregon Coast properties.

"The Lodge," as many employees and local residents referred to the resort, would define careers, not only of the three principals but of later managers and long-time employees. With the sale of the Lodge in 1997 the era was over, ended by corporate insensitivity and new managers without the slightest concept of the amazing coming together of creative forces which built the resort 30 years ago.

Salishan was the first of its kind—and perhaps the last. Tight environmental laws, a changing demographic mix and a struggling economy practically guarantee there won't be a repeat.

Barbara Fealy died in 2001, John Storrs died in 2003. John Gray is in his 80s. A bronze plate with their names, rescued from the remodeling rubble of the first corporate buyer of Salishan Lodge in 1997, now greets visitors entering the Lodge's massive front door. But the aura of Salishan Lodge, the Mobil Five-Stars, the long-term employees and the resort's casual elegance which sprouted from one man's vision may be lost forever.

CHAPTER ONE

The Siletz

"The future of Oregon's estuaries depends on the care and effort which go into the planning and development process now. Many of Oregon's estuaries are still in a near-pristine state and in no instance has an estuary deteriorated to the point where we do not have the ability to plan its future development."

William Cox, Director,
Oregon Division of State Lands
June 1973

"The Siletz Bay area has been substantially modified by human activities."

Environmental Assessment
Proposed Siletz Bay National Wildlife Refuge
October 1990

William Cox believed many of Oregon's estuaries were still in a "near-pristine state" in 1973 but, even though Siletz Bay was only 60 miles from his Oregon Division of State Lands office in Salem, perhaps he hadn't visited the estuary in recent years. Man-made dikes altered the river's seasonal floods; tons of fill dirt were dumped into the bay creating waterfront homesites; stranded logs mired in the low-tide mud of "Snag Alley," the result of a collapsed dam in Valsetz and logging in the 1920s and 1930s. Siletz Bay and the estuary have been significantly altered. Sediment has smothered the once productive softshell clam beds. On the sand spit overlooking those alterations are the homes of Salishan.

Siletz Bay's delicate estuarine ecology faced another bizarre scheme in the early 1960s. With the right combination of funding an airport runway–3,200 feet long, 500-feet wide-- would have lined the bay's shoreline with a connecting dike road from Highway 101.

A meeting in 1963 with representatives from the State Board of Aeronautics set in motion plans to build an airport on the spit and into the bay. Filling a portion of Siletz Bay for an airport runway wouldn't happen today with the myriad of environmental restrictions, but in 1963 the discussion with state and county officials included that possibility as well as building the dike road skirting the estuary to the proposed airport from Siletz Keys. Engineering drawings for the road were sent out for review.

As late as September 1963 Oregon officials were still considering the possibility of the Siletz Bay airport and Salishan Properties offered property on the Siletz Spit for the project. The State of Oregon committed up to $50,000 for the airport development, the Port of Newport agreed to $10,000, grants from the FAA, and $25,000 in road construction assistance from Lincoln County went into the financial mix. Robert Dunn, state director of aeronautics, said the project would be "an airport which would include a 2,600 foot landing strip competing with the likes of the Nut Tree in California and Ocean Shores in Washington." Estimated price tag was $225,000, later raised to more than $300,000, most of it in federal dollars.

In 1964 R.S. Livermore, general manager of the Salishan Properties, said the airport topic "...is still very much alive" and a causeway road from Highway 101 to the airport would create a large permanent lake "of at least 100 acres"...which would be ideal for fishing, sailing and boating."

Withdrawal of federal funds put the project on hold and the spit airport idea faded, replaced by the current airport south of Salishan Lodge. Construction of that airport began in 1967 and officially opened in 1971. Close call for the estuary.

MILLPORT SLOUGH

Drainage from 373 square miles of watershed translates into the natural floods of winter as the Siletz River morphs into a brown torrent. With the man-made alterations in the estuary the rising, rapidly flowing waters take a direct shot at the east side of Siletz Spit instead of dissipating in the sloughs. As a result, erosion on the spit forced additional altering of the estuary as tons of rip-rap (large boulders) were dumped to protect the pricey Salishan properties from sliding into the bay, a scenario similar to the west side as the ocean carved into the foredunes. The Spit was caught in a watery vise–and still is.

Millport Slough is the navigable south channel of the Siletz River. But when a condemned bridge was demolished by Lincoln County in 1951 the solution was fill and a dike road. The project cut the flow of additional fresh water into the estuary, allowing tons more silt as the flushing action of the fresh water was diminished, and rearranged the flood patterns, channeling flows against the Siletz Spit. Farmland was created as the flow through the estuary was diverted.

In the early 1970s Dr. Wallace Baldinger, a Salishan resident, formed an organization called Citizens for Revitalizing Siletz Bay. The Millport Slough dike was a target and Baldinger, armed with a petition containing 150 signatures, put the slough in his cross-hairs. A county solution of installing an eight-foot wide culvert met with resistance. One reported incident recalls an angry farmer's wife, Ruby Jackson, with a gun, preventing county crews from installing the culvert, fearing the flooding of her reclaimed pastureland. A less exciting rendition has the county attorney claiming the culvert wasn't installed due to a threatened lawsuit. Whatever happened, the culvert sat on top of the dike road and was never installed. Enter the State of Oregon.

In 1974 the Oregon Division of State Lands (DSL) ordered the dike removed and the area restored to the natural habitat, the first time in history the state had exercised its powers for estuarine protection. Meanwhile, Dr. Baldinger and his group, now known as SOS (Save our Siletz), an abbreviation improvement over SOB (Save Our Bay), met to discuss the Siletz Bay situation. The group disbanded within a short period of time. By late 1974 Lincoln County, at a cost of $50,000, built a timber bridge over the slough. At 16 feet wide and 150 feet long, the bridge allowed the Millport Slough waters to again mix into the estuary. But by then flows were still too weak to flush the bay's built-up sediment into the Pacific.

Estuaries are delicate, marine life entering the estuarine zone as salt water mixes with the fresh waters of the rivers and creeks. Twice a day the tides force nutrients and oxygen into the bay as solar radiation easily penetrates the shallow water and spurs the rapid growth of aquatic vegetation. Tidelands offer a home for burrowing creatures. Eelgrass in the Siletz Bay provides habitat for 25 species of ducks, three species of geese as well as Great

Blue Herons. The food chain begins with microscopic phytoplankton, zooplankton and small crustaceans.

"Formed from drowned river valleys at the end of the ice ages, they (estuaries) are environments out of equilibrium," said Paul Komar in his book, "The Pacific Northwest Coast."

"Most estuaries are eventually reduced to channels that transport all of the river sediments to the ocean. However, such a development takes thousands of years, so we should not view our estuaries as temporary features."

Siletz Bay, 128 miles south of the Columbia River, is a small blip on Oregon's estuary radar screen with only 1,187 acres, most of that, 775 acres, in tideland acres. The estuary is designated "conservation" under Oregon's classification system. Compared with the Columbia River estuary at 93,000 plus acres or Coos Bay at 12,380 acres, Siletz Bay is 10th in size of the 17 Oregon estuaries. But the small size doesn't diminish the remarkable array of fish and fowl; peregrine falcons, egrets, herons, Red-Tailed hawks, brown pelicans, bald eagles, Canadian geese, as well as dozens of fish species. Chinook and Coho salmon travel through the estuary enroute to spawning grounds far up the Siletz River or Drift Creek or Schooner Creek, a dangerous voyage the moment the fish enter the bay as more than 150 hungry harbor seals perch on the tip of Siletz Spit or prowl at high tide through Snag Alley to await the fresh morsels.

The Siletz River is second in Oregon to the Columbia River in importance for spawning of cutthroat trout. Among Oregon rivers the Siletz is ranked third for Coho salmon, fourth for summer steelhead, fifth for Chinook salmon, and eighth for winter steelhead. Dungeness crabs scurry along the estuary bottom, sweeping in on the high tides. Lured by fish heads or rotting fish carcasses many of the crabs find their way to the crab rings set out by the recreational crabbers. Fishermen are rewarded with perch, rockfish or an occasional flounder. Soft-shell clams can be harvested in the mud and gravel along the bay's edge near Drift Creek. Large numbers of waterfowl either winter on the bay or use the bay as a pit stop on long migrations.

With its salt marsh, brackish marsh, mudflats, tidal creeks and sloughs Siletz Bay is a vital link in the ecology of the Central Oregon Coast as the waters from the Siletz River, Drift Creek and Schooner Creek (reportedly named for a small schooner which ran aground in the late 1800s) dump fresh water into the mix.

Seawater pushes up the creeks and rivers, reaching 2 miles upstream at Schooner and Drift Creeks from the highway while the tidewater at high tide for the Siletz River is 24 miles east from Highway 101.

At the narrow channel or "jaws" the Pacific breakers crash relentlessly against the beach, scraping away the sand during the winter months and replenishing the beaches in the summer. Navigation is discouraged, the shallow channel and currents making crossing the entrance a foolhardy adventure. The schooner "Calumet," delivering 30 tons of flour for the Coast Indian Reservation in 1856, discovered the ferocity of both the entrance to the bay and winter storms. As the ship was beached on Dec. 8, 1856, crews tried to unload the cargo, only to be met by a "heavy blow from the west," described as the worst in 20 years, which destroyed the entire cargo and swept Indian houses and the residents into the churning waters.

DEVELOPING THE BAY

"Revitalization" of Siletz Bay or, by another term, commercialization of Siletz Bay, has had reincarnations, some of them triggered by the Salishan development and the desire for increased recreational facilities as well as pressure to compete with other Oregon bays. While the idea of ocean-going barges routinely being pushed through Siletz Bay and over the bar seems a fantasy today, the giant log rafts of the 1930s carried an estimated one quarter million board feet of lumber to distant ports. With the world's heaviest growth of Sitka spruce in the Siletz River watershed at 150,000 board feet per acre, the timber industry boomed. Many of the logs stranded today in Siletz Bay came from those boom years. It all stopped in 1938 as the last of the log rafts crossed the bar and the log trucks took over, the result of Highway 101 and the river bridges.

Serious consideration of Siletz Bay development began in 1968. The U.S. Army Corps of Engineers, with a resolution from the U.S. Senate and pressure from a local group formed seven years earlier called the Siletz Bay Improvement Committee with some funding from Salishan Properties Inc., held the first public hearing on the issue. T.J.Murray and Associates, a consulting engineering company under contract from the Port of Newport

(Siletz Bay was included in the Port of Newport boundaries), presented plans for a $6 million dollar "improvement".

Endorsed by a Portland-based barge company, local and national politicians, the plan met zero resistance. Citing the most important reason for harbor development as providing barge carrier service for the bulk movement of timber products, the plan included a basin for turning barges and mooring commercial fishing boats (the plan's cost would rise to $8 million by 1972). During the same hearing Lincoln City Mayor Ross Evans, emphasizing the growth of Lincoln City, predicted a population of 10,000 or more within 3 to 5 years. According to the 2000 census, the population of Lincoln City is 7,437, a few thousand shy of the Evans' prediction 32 years previous.

The Army Corps of Engineers in July 1973 issued a report stressing "the need exists for small boat moorage facilities in Siletz Bay," but the report didn't recommend those "improvements" because of "lack of economic justification."

Improvements "needed" included a 3,000 foot north jetty, a 2,000 foot south jetty, the harbor entrance dredged to 250-feet wide and 14 feet deep, and a mooring basin between Drift Creek and the Siletz River. A 1,200-ft. long causeway from Highway 101 to the moorage was also noted.

Salishan leaseholders were dead-set against any jetty plans as the shifting sand deposits caused by the jetty could have significant impact on the Spit, according to the leaseholders.

The "revitalization" of Siletz Bay, even with a cold shoulder from the Army Corps of Engineers, wouldn't die quietly. A steering committee met in November 1973 with 32 persons interested in the project. Again, no action resulted from the meetings.

Coast Guard patrols of the bay ended years ago due to boating inactivity. Ebb tides create hazardous conditions for any boater near the river's mouth. Over the years discussion of jetties, boat basins, and other developments in the bay went nowhere. Recreational boating in Siletz Bay was often discussed but, to this day, the bay remains shallow and undeveloped. Efforts at forming the Port of Siletz failed in 1977 by a 681 to 492 margin, a 20% turnout of the 5,239 eligible voters. North Lincoln County voters weren't in any mood for port districts after withdrawing from the Port of Newport in 1972, a vote resulting in the resignation of long-time port chairman Lyle Hasselbrink of Lincoln City.

City work crews in 1992 dug out the sand on the Taft beach another 8 feet in efforts to replicate the beach level 25 years previous as excess sand was piling up on S. 51st Street. City officials said a "flood of sand" was choking Siletz Bay.

A Lincoln City public forum in 1993 drew 163 residents to city hall in another effort to discuss a port for Siletz Bay.

In 2005 another group "Save Oregon's Shores" (SOS)-- formed as a 501 (c) 3 corporation to promote changing the Siletz Bay "natural estuary" designation to allow a range of activities from logging transportation to recreational boating. The group is already facing substantial opposition to the plan.

SILETZ KEYS, THE BRIDGE AND THE WILDLIFE REFUGE

Estuaries are the most productive biological regions on earth. But the estuaries and their proximity to the Pacific Ocean also lure the developers with their plans of fill-and-build. Homesite sales and access are only a few hundred truckloads of dirt away. Siletz Bay didn't escape the developers.

"Abusive land management in the (Siletz) watershed has caused excessive siltation resulting in lowering of salinity", according to William Wicks in his OSU Marine Advisory Program publication "Crisis in Oregon Estuaries." "Now the danger is filling."

A major fill was Siletz Keys, a housing development at the north end of the bay formed by dredging and then filling in the bay, raising the level of 80 acres to highway height. The U.S. Army Corps of Engineers issued a permit for the dredge and fill operations in 1965. The developer, H.G. Palmberg, in partnership with Loyd Calkins, sold 38 homesites on the "new" land in addition to building an access road from Highway 101 across the estuary. It was only the beginning as artist's renditions and sales material showed a Florida-type development with inlets, canals and 200 homesites. Application to the U.S. Army Corps of Engineers for expansion of Siletz Keys went public in 1971 and more than 100 Salishan residents voiced strong opposition. The Palmberg group would only complete phase one before Gov. Tom McCall issued a moratorium on the granting of permits for estuary filling or dredging in 1972. Siletz Keys was doomed. The 38 homesite owners on the only two completed streets---Trout Place and Keys Place---- won't have to worry about additional neighbors in the future.

Oregon agencies including the Oregon Fish Commission also disapproved of additional Siletz Bay estuary fills including additional acreage purchase requests from the Palmberg/Calkins group to, in Palmberg's description, "square off property lines."

Another major blockage of fresh water into the bay came from the Oregon Department of Transportation (ODOT) with construction of the new, $4 million four-lane Highway 101 bridge over the Siletz River, a replacement for the Conde McCullough-designed bridge constructed in the early 1920s. The proposed bridge was originally penciled out at 80-feet vertical clearance above mean high water to allow barges to travel up the river. That plan was dismissed after several complaints including the board of directors of Salishan Leaseholders Inc. (SLI). Substantial fill was dumped into the estuary for the bridge approaches as Highway 101 was realigned and the fill effectively blocked some freshwater flows. The bridge opened in late summer 1973 with a 30-foot clearance. One state official in 1980 called the bridge "...one of the worst examples of natural resource destruction around."

In Newport, a coastal town 25-miles south of Siletz Bay, Roy W. Lowe, a biologist with the U.S. Fish and Wildlife Service (USFWS), had written an article for the Oregon Coast Aquarium newsletter. The proposed aquarium was soliciting donations and other funding for construction. Lowe's article concerned the coastal wildlife sanctuaries, none of which included estuaries. John Gray read the article and contacted Lowe with an offer to donate nearly 46 acres which Gray owned as the first step in formation of a Siletz Bay National Wildlife refuge.

National wildlife refuges began in 1903 when President Theodore Roosevelt gave formal protection to Florida Island, a breeding area for brown pelicans.

Recognizing the need for protection of the Siletz estuary the federal government agreed to Gray's proposal and formed the refuge in 1991 with further land acquisition under the authority of the Migratory Bird Conservation Act of 1929, the Fish and Wildlife Act of 1956, and the Emergency Wetland Resources Act of 1986. Acquisition funding would be provided with funds from the Land and Water Conservation Fund Act of 1965. With a total of 1,936 acres proposed for the refuge the USFSW has purchased

525 acres including an additional 146 acres from John Gray ($180,880) and another 64 acres from Gray's daughter, Janet Webster. Of those 1,936 acres the State of Oregon owns 1,060 in tidelands. Thus, with approximately 876 acres originally in private hands, the USFSW has already purchased 525 acres and continues to negotiate with the remaining owners for continued expansion of the refuge.

Primary goal of the refuge, according to the agency, was to allow the salt marsh to return to its naturally tidal influenced condition. In the fall of 2002 a partnership consisting of (USFWS), Ducks Unlimited and the Confederated Tribes of the Siletz Indians restored 86 acres of tidal marsh. The project breached 220 feet of dike, removing two dikes totaling 9,300 feet and filling 1,200 feet of artificial ditches. Woody debris was placed in the marsh to improve habitat for anadromous fish.

Siletz Bay was designated as an "Important Bird Area" by the Audubon Society in 2005

On the western edge of the bay is Siletz Spit. Later known as Salishan Spit, the narrow spit would anchor the homes of some of Oregon's rich and famous.

ALEUTIAN LOW & PACIFIC HIGH

Cape Foulweather, Cape Meares, Cape Perpetua, Yaquina Head,; the coastal Oregon headlands poke igneous basalt chins into the Pacific and take the winter storms' uppercuts. Winds, often gusting to 100 miles per hour, push the drenching rains eastward. In the winter months, the Aleutian Low's waves of cold collide with the Pacific marine air and dust the Coast Range with a few inches of snow before dropping into the Willamette Valley and depositing more rain.

Pushing eastward the storms sweep up the Cascade Mountains' western front where, to the skiers' delight, most of the moisture is squeezed from the nimbostratus and stratus clouds as snow. The high desert east side of the Cascades is left starved for moisture.

The differences? Otis (Oregon Coast), average of 97 inches of rainfall per year; Portland (Willamette Valley), 43 inches; Government Camp (Cascades), 87 inches; Burns (Eastern Oregon) 10 inches; all of this in a range of less than 300 miles.

The "Pineapple Express," a subtropical flow of moisture, can toss a wrench into the winter pattern, bringing copious amounts of moisture to the Coast, warmer temperatures to the Cascade snowpack and, in some cases, statewide flooding. Arctic polar air chills the central and eastern parts of the state during the winter, cold wisps sneaking westward through the Columbia River Gorge and crashing head-on into the Pacific moisture, bringing the Willamette Valley, especially Portland, freezing rain and snow.

On the central Oregon Coast, Lincoln County beckons the elements, taking the first hit as the Pacific storms and chains of rain batter the sparsely populated county. Racing eastward as often as every three days in the peak months of November and December, the one-day storms whip the surf into a frenzy, dumping logs and sand on some highways, depositing knee-deep foam on the long, deserted stretches of beach and sending horizontal rain squalls bumping against the Coast Range. The 20-foot high ocean waves scratch and claw at the beaches and sand dunes, swallowing sand and sometimes houses, later returning the course sand as the summer currents move northward.

Polar air rarely reaches the Coast, the area with the smallest temperature range in Oregon–less than 15 degrees year around. Coastal residents are as surprised by the occasional 90-degree summer day as by a winter freeze or a snowy day which sends kids home from school and drivers into a tizzy.

Midwestern transplants shake their heads at the chaos one inch or less of the white stuff generates. Coastal drivers try to figure out tire chains. Snowmen make the local newspaper's front page, photos of the local bank thermometer at 30 degrees make page two. The snow is gone in 48 hours although a snowfall in 1968 gave the Coast 18 inches of snow which stayed on the ground for more than a week.

Winter is continual cloud cover. Pacific winter storm systems line up in the jet stream and wait their turn to pummel the coast. Breathless TV weather forecasters in Portland give us "high wind warnings" and "high surf warnings" for the Coast as if the stormy weather is a 21st century phenomenon.

"Weather cams" on top of coastal hotels, shaking and coated with raindrops, give the Valley People televised glimpses of coastal storms. Some storm watchers gather at coastal overlooks, observing their annual rites of winter. Portland weather personalities pose on the Coast in logoed Columbia Sportswear parkas as raindrops spot the camera lens and gale force winds echo through their hand-held microphones. Meanwhile, long-time coastal residents shrug or barely notice.

And then it's spring. Crocuses pop through coastal sloughs, blackberry vines spring to life, daffodils paint the coastal hills yellow.

Summer's Pacific high pressure brings a daily afternoon north wind and the accompanying ocean upwelling, a coastal feature which pushes warmer water away from the shore, replaced by nutrient-rich cooler water. Sea life thrives.

THE SILETZ

Origin of the Siletz River name has many interpretations. From an Indian maiden name of "Celeste" to a Chinook language name for fern river–"Siletz-Chuck"–to another Indian word "Tsa Shna'dsch amin", the Siletz name appears to have a wide range of historical origins. Spellings have ranged from "Celeetz" to "Selitz" to "Salitz." Another origin cites the Rogue River Indians as applying the name "Silis" meaning black bear. But whatever the spelling or pronunciation, the Siletz River has played an important role in the area's ecology, tourism and history.

Bubbling out of the Coast Range approximately 72 miles from the ocean mouth, the Siletz River, the crookedest river in Oregon, drains more than 300 square miles as it follows a path from its source at the 2,850 Coast Range elevation to the ocean. In 1991 the river was named one of Oregon's 10 most endangered rivers based on "decimated" fish stocks. The Oregon Rivers Council targeted logging, grazing, road building as well as over-fishing as main causes for depleted fish populations

At an average flow of 1,930 cubic feet per second (cfs) at the mouth, the river can rapidly reach flood stage as the coastal winter storms dump copious amount of rain in the Coast Range. A November 1909 measurement recorded 34,500 cfs. Recorded minimum was 48 cfs (1965 and 1967).As the river ends its journey at Siletz Bay, the currents swirl against Siletz Spit on the western bay boundary. It was on this narrow band of sand that Salishan began.

Beachfront. Blocks from the beach. Near the beach. Real estate agents tout "the beach" as a selling tool. Buyers, most with above average incomes, seek those properties, often for second homes only used on occasional weekends or family gatherings. The Salishan beachfront homes command top dollar. Supply and demand at its finest. Some are weekend rentals, subject to tight restrictions. But as the expensive dwellings crowd the oceanfront lots, the beaches remain public. Beach access may be challenging as is the case with Salishan. A muddy trail, neglected in recent years by the corporate owners and barely marked, starts behind the former Chevron station (now a trendy spa under the new ownership of 2004) at the Marketplace shopping center, follows the golf course, and eventually leads to the beach. Guests at Salishan Lodge can use an entry card for the Salishan entry gate and drive through the development along Salishan Drive to a parking lot at the end of the Spit.

The public can also gain access to the Salishan beach by parking at Gleneden Beach State Park and walking the beach more than three miles north to the Salishan beach. Once there the mostly vacant Salishan houses, shades pulled,, range in size and shape but meet the architectural guidelines. No double-wides or manufactured houses here. The oceanfront property is kept out of the Pacific with piled rip-rap, the only defense against the capricious rip tides and winter storms which batter the spit and tear away at the foredunes. There are access points from the beach to Salishan Drive although a security guard may give you a second look if you're wandering through the development. Streets are private. The beach is usually deserted.

Oregonians are used to public beaches and may even take them for granted. A visit to other states with beach access limitations and privatization should be a reminder that the beaches could have been lost had it not been for a few politicians and activists.

The beaches were natural highways, connecting rural areas of the coast. First by horseback, later by the automobile, the beach was the perfect road. In the late 1800s the State of Oregon did sell some tidal shore to private owners, but it became obvious this wasn't the best of ideas as it could restrict the "highway." It was Oregon's 14th governor, Oswald West, who saw the selling of tidal shores as a poor idea. West pushed through the plan to designate all beaches as public highways between the Columbia River and the California state line. But, as would later be discovered, the exact boundaries of the beach were in dispute.

BEACH BOUNDARIES

"Dry sand," the area beyond the ordinary high tide mark, could still be in private ownership and was in some cases. Legislation in 1965 designating beaches as state recreation areas pinpointed the area seaward of the ordinary high tide mark. The area between the high tide mark and the vegetation line was open for development. A Cannon Beach motel owner, William Hay, tested the state with a fenced area on the beach and a designation of a private beach. The action raised numerous issues and one politician, Gov. Tom McCall, jumped into the debate.

Introduction of the "Beach Bill" in 1967 triggered immediate political opposition and only a series of newspaper and television features exposed the issue to the public. Oregonians responded with thousands of letters and phone calls, a close call as the bill was close to being tabled after developers got the attention of lawmakers. The public outrage had an effect. Gov.McCall walked along several beaches including Salishan in attempting to form a formula for establishing boundaries of the beach. McCall and his staff came up with 16 feet above the sea level markers established by the U.S. Coast Guard and Geodetic Survey.

Recalling the event in his autobiography, McCall described the first visit to the Salishan beach for a measurement.

"The tide was all the way out, and an oceanographer took a slender, 16-foot pole down to the water's edge and set it down exactly perpendicular," according to one of the oceanographers. "Where the string running horizontal from the top of the pole landward touches down should be the vegetation line."

According to McCall, the 16-foot marker "delineated the people's own beach all the way from Washington state south to California."

A House committee agreed on the 16-foot elevation with a 5.7 ft. plus 300 feet at estuaries. McCall signed the bill on July 6, 1967. More sophisticated surveys set the beach boundaries with more precision and would be incorporated into a 1969 bill which

McCall also signed.

Coincidentally, the first development allowed by the State Highway Commission on the newly protected beach was the Inn at Spanish Head in Lincoln City.

In her 1977 book "Oregon Beaches: A Birthright Preserved" author Kathryn A. Straton, a state employee with the Historic Preservation Section of the Oregon Parks and Recreation Branch, made the following observations:

"Oregon was ready for the Beach Law. And the process from which the law evolved has been as significant as the Beach Law itself," Straton wrote. "The events thrust a relatively young and

Postcard view of Siletz Bay and Taft from the 1950s.

environmentally vulnerable state through an emotionally and politically wrenching experience. Yet, Oregonians emerged more mature and more confident of the worth of the democratic process."

It was the beach which brought the developers to the Oregon Coast including John D. Gray.

Advertising brochure for Siletz Keys.
Area outlined on right was the only completed development.
Area highlighted on left was proposed airport runway.

CHAPTER 2

Discovery

"A chain of lofty breakers extends from shore to shore directly across the outlet of the Celeetz bay, which I think would be impossible for any kind of vessel or boat to pass in safety."

Lt. Theodore Talbot

Lieutenant Theodore Talbot first saw the area now known as the Salishan Spit and described it as a "...range of loose sandhills." Talbot may have been the first to document another fact now well-known to Oregonians; summer on the Coast can be "unreasonably chilly and very misty, much more resembling mid-winter than the height of summer." Welcome to the Oregon Coast, Ted.

More than 100 years later those "sandhills" would anchor foundations for Oregon summer homes, homes not for the coastal residents, many of whom existed on minimum wages from tourist business jobs, but for the movers and shakers of the Willamette Valley; a summer residence for Phil Knight while away from his Nike empire in the Portland suburb of Beaverton, tasteful residences of Portland lawyers, business owners and executives, physicians, and those on the fringe of stock and bond wheelings and dealings. Houses would be rented to Paul Newman and other movie stars during the filming of Oregonian author Ken Kesey's "Sometimes a Great Notion." A TV series, "Knots Landing," would use the area for a location shoot.

The architectural committees made sure the residences met a set criteria. No Ticky-Tacky-By-the-Sea. Paint colors, roofs, fencing and other accents went through the committee for final approval.

It was the Oregon status symbol, the 'beach house". The 1960s status came not at Gearhart or Seaside or Lincoln City but on those loose sandhills rising on the shorelines of Siletz Bay and the Pacific Ocean, shorelines later disappearing at an alarming rate.

Described by some at the time as mansions, the houses hardly qualify today in the mega-room, mega square-foot "beach cabins" with views of Haystack Rock in Cannon Beach, or those built on the slip-sliding cliffs of Cape Meares. Complementing the housing was a resort to the east and across Highway 101, one which hosted movie stars on clandestine weekend getaways, state governors, and generations of Northwest families.

SALISHAN-THE NAME

The name didn't roll off the tongue easily. Many put an "h" in front of the first "a" to make it "Shalishan." A popular working-class tavern nearby would later mock the name to "Salishack." Some disgruntled employees in the later corporate era called it "Salisham."

Most people had never heard the term Salishan, a fact which gave the original developer pause to consider changing it to the easily recognizable but boring "Sea Ridge" or "Oceanview".

Early evidence showed Indian habitation on the Oregon Coast as long as 8,000 to 10,000 years ago, but the ocean has now covered earlier relics just as it covered the land bridge from Siberia to North America. New evidence unearthed in 2002 at Oregon's Boardman State Park lends credence to the theory that early inhabitants arrived by sea. Whether by land or by sea, the debate continues. But by the mid-1800s Indian land would vanish, buried under government giveaways and broken treaties. Many of the Indians had already died from numerous diseases brought to shore by the white explorers.

From Siberia across the land bridge or by sea, the early inhabitants were hunters, settling the coastal areas last. Later, tribes of the Tillamook, Nehalem, Siletz and Alsea tribes harvested the clams, mussels and crabs from the seashore, gathered the camas, blueberries, blackberries and huckleberries, unaware of the battles less than 200 miles inland.

Coastal rivers teemed with salmon and steelhead.

Estuaries such as Siletz Bay provided hunting grounds as flocks of geese and ducks fed in the marshy estuary. Cedar trees provided material for necessities such as shelter, canoes and clothing. Fire-hardened Spruce tree roots were sculpted into spear points and arrowheads.

Languages were as varied as the tribes. On the central Oregon Coast the Tillamook and Siletz were grouped into the Salishan Linguistic Isolate but, even with the same language grouping, there were differences. The Salishan, or Salish, families encompassed tribes in Montana, northern Idaho and Washington, and British Columbia as well as the coastal tribes.

EARLY EXPLORATION

Coastal Oregon was the baby in Northwest exploration, untouched by whites. From the deck of the "Resolution", Captain James Cook first saw Yaquina Bay in 1778 and named Cape Foulweather (for obvious reasons!) and Cape Perpetua near Yachats, named for Saint Perpetua, the Christian martyr murdered on March 7, the same day Cook spotted the Cape. There is no evidence Cook set foot on land along the central Oregon Coast on his northward journey. But his voyages opened the door to exploration and the eventual white settlements. The voyage of Robert Gray in 1792 discovered the Columbia River which would later become a basis for American claims to the Oregon Territory. Spanish galleons may have skirted the Oregon Coast much earlier.

The Oregon Coast needed land exploration. Trappers such as Alexander McLeod, chief trader from the Hudsons Bay Company crossed the Salmon River and stayed at Devils Lake in what is now Lincoln City before moving on due to a shortage of beavers.

With the Oregon Territory formed in 1848 following the infamous Whitman murders by Indians in Walla Walla, Washington, the door opened for exploration.

The Oregon Coast was the last frontier for the westward United States expansion. As a result of the lack of detailed maps the Coast kept a low profile. Agricultural land was scarce and settlers didn't flock to the Coast. Indian wars raged to the southeast as the Rogues found the new white settlers a threat to their lands. Discovery of gold added to the Oregon rush. Political pressure for additional white land was building, land which the Indians claimed as theirs. The desirable valleys were the target, valleys framed by the Coast Range and the Cascades with rich topsoil and moderate rainfall. The Coast wasn't considered for settlement but it was good enough for the Indians as would later be shown.

THE TALBOT EXPLORATION

Theodore Talbot was born in Kentucky, eventually rising to the ranks of Major and Assistant Adjutant General in 1861. He was assigned as part of the second expedition of Capt. John C. Fremont from St. Louis to the lower Columbia River, coming back to the Northwest in 1848 after the formation of the Oregon Territory and assigned to Ft. Vancouver.

By the time General Persifor F. Smith of Ft. Vancouver and commander of the military forces on the Pacific Coast assigned Talbot, a first lieutenant, to the coastal exploration, the number of Indians in the Siletz River basin and on the Oregon Coast had been decimated by wars, fires and diseases brought by the white men in their ships. The Siletz band was considered a southern branch of the Tillamook although later the river and tribe went by the same name. Present day Indians are called Siletz but are a mix of several different Indian bands.

Lt. Talbot set out on his expedition with a sergeant and nine men, the sergeant later taking ill and returning to Vancouver. The rush to the gold fields of California left supplies difficult to obtain but Talbot finally left Oregon City on August 20, 1849 and began a circuitous route to the Oregon coast in search of coal. Crossing the Coast Range Talbot's expedition dropped into the Siletz Valley "surrounded on all sides by tall forest of pine, spruce, hemlock, etc."

Talbot's detachment did find coal in the Siletz Valley, a small find but one which gave Talbot optimism that later explorers would find larger deposits.

Talbot observed no Indians on the river, at least in the Siletz Valley.

Talbot's expedition took him through the mountains to Yaquina Bay., south to Alsea Bay and then turning north again, reaching the shores of Siletz Bay on September 5, "a disagreeably cold day."

Talbot described Siletz Bay as a vast marsh and, on the west side, "a range of loose sandhills" and the bay bordered by a "great number" of Indian canoes with the dead, an Indian tradition.

Talbot further described the west shore of the bay as about three and one-half miles long with the greatest width as one mile.

"A chain of lofty breakers extends from shore to shore directly across the outlet of the Celeetz bay, which I think would be impossible for any kind of vessel or boat to pass in safety."

Losing a horse to the breakers at the entrance of Siletz Bay Talbot decided to build a raft of drift logs, finding out soon enough that this wasn't going to be an easy task and, instead, substituting a large Indian canoe to cross the river. Talbot found a lone Indian who told Talbot that two Indians and their families were the only residents of the bay, "the last lingering remnants of a large population which once dwelt upon these waters." The "mortality" of 1831, as Talbot described it, apparently spread south and decimated the coastal tribes.

Talbot returned to Ft. Vancouver on September 15th. On the Oregon Coast the small numbers of remaining Indian tribes would later be joined by hundreds of Indians as the Coast Reservation came into existence.

THE VALLEYS

Willamette, Rogue, Umpqua; valleys sandwiched between the Coast Range and the Cascades. It was here the white settlers of the 1800s claimed their land. But the land already had residents and the settlers' unofficial eviction notices would set in motion conflicts leading to the Indian tribes being transported hundreds of miles away to a strange land on the Oregon Coast. As verdant valleys were left behind, the tribes would endure desperation and a lifestyle ill-suited to their traditions and heritage.

Gold fever could strike anywhere. So could homesteading fever. In the Rogue River valley of Oregon, the fortune seekers and homesteaders came in droves in the mid-1850s and increasing hostilities erupted between them and the Indians, hostilities eventually forcing the U.S. government to remove the Indians from their homelands.

Coastal Indians rarely traveled further than 25 miles from their rivers as coastal headlands and pounding surf limited coastal trade and travel. Their cedar canoes didn't venture into the vast Pacific. Satisfied with the rich bounty of fish and game, the coastal Indians maintained a peaceful existence. Trappers ventured into the uncharted territory in the early 1800s. Diseases brought by white Europeans to the north had taken their toll on the Indian villages.

It was a different story across the Coast Range in the Oregon valleys. Westward migration, fueled by US Government land grants and the discovery of gold in the Rogue River Valley, brought the Indians and whites face to face and the resulting hostilities forced a showdown, ones which the Indians would lose along with their homelands and traditions.

First known as the Coast Reservation, later as the Siletz Reservation, the 1.4 million acres, sprawled 100 miles between Cape Lookout in present-day Tillamook County on the north and an area between the Siuslaw and Umpqua Rivers on the south and inland 20 miles, an area the size of Delaware. The reservation was created by Presidential executive order in November 1855.

Joel Palmer, the second superintendent of Indian Affairs for Washington and Oregon, made the decision to keep the reservation on the west side of the Coast Range, reasoning that the Coast Range would protect the Indians from white interference. The land was also less valuable than the rich Willamette Valley.

A Siletz agency office was established near the present day town of Siletz and relocation of the Oregon Indians began. Another reservation, the Grand Ronde, was formed on the east side of the Coast Range.

The relocation of more than 40 different tribes and more than 2,000 Indians began by sea and by land, many of the Indians becoming seasick on the sea trip northward. Some were forced to walk more than 100 miles as the native homelands and lifestyles were left behind, all part of a plan by the U.S Government to train the Indians to become self-supporting farmers.

The Siletz Reservation was "home" to 2,025 Indians from various tribes. Diseases such as TB, syphillis and bronchitis decimated the tribes and by the time of land allocation in 1887 only about 600 Indians survived from the Siletz area. Internal conflicts between the different tribes created constant strife.

Poor living conditions further antagonized the remaining Indians.

An Indian agent described tribal members on the reservation as "wretchedly poor and destitute of all the necessities and comforts of life except what is supplied them by the government." Another description called the reservation "...as bleak a place as any interment camp."

LAND FOR SALE

In the Oregon interior valleys the white settlers were grabbing more land and suddenly the coastal property, designated as the Siletz Resevation, was looking more desirable. A wagon road from Corvallis to Yaquina Bay brought more activity to the Coast, bolstered by a booming oyster business on Yaquina Bay.

In December 1865 President Andrew Johnson signed an order giving Yaquina Bay to white settlement and 10 years later the land south of the Alsea Bay was also opened for white settlement. The tribes received $16,500 in compensation for the Yaquina Bay land. The only remaining portion of the reservation was north Lincoln County and the Grande Ronde agency in Polk County

The General Allotment Act of 1887, a government plan to give land to Indians, authorized allocating approximately 80 acres to all tribal members with the rest of the land, so-called "surplus", 175,000 acres, for the white settler. Approximately 44,000 acres went to 551 tribal members. By the early 1900s, one half of the land been sold and was no longer held by tribal members. The remaining land, with the exception of a small strip between Lincoln City and Newport, was opened for white settlement. Within the span of 40 years, more than 1 million acres were taken from the Indians despite numerous treaties and agreements. The Siletz tribe received $142,600 from the U.S. Government for the 175, 000 acres opened for homesteading. The federal government would terminate recognition of the Siletz tribe in 1956, reversing that decision in 1977.

In 1894 the property where Salishan Lodge and the Salishan development are now sited was allocated to "...an Indian of the Siletz Reservation", five Indians to be exact. Property went to Alsea Johnson, Edward Wilson, Lucy Wilson, George Stanton and Ollie Stanton, a total of more than 400 acres in the form of trust patents.

Other property owned by the U.S Government was available for homesteading at $1.50 per acre. Coastal land was now for sale.

Fifty years ago, this wasn't called a "city"
It was eight small coastal towns and villages
Road's End, Neotsu, Wecoma, Oceanlake
Nelscott, Taft, Cutler City and Gleneden Beach
Strung along twenty miles of seacoast reach
Here was a share of Eden's beauty

Red and white variegated daisies
And strawberries grew wild
In our cottage yard
and in the pre-dawn morning fog
Small rabbits came to feed
Silverspot butterflies fluttered in the sun
And one morning, up early
To fish for pinkfin perch
I saw a cougar
(Yes, a cougar–I checked the pawprints to be sure!)
Lope along the beach
I have never seen another

Across the road old Captain Lundy
Gazed through seaward-facing windows
And pondered the ocean's timeless quandary
When the westward setting sun
Painted Lundy's parlor orange-red, he
Would tell the children how it had been
Before his retirement from the sea

From our kitchen window to the north
Could be seen
Cascade Head enshrouded in mist
And ancient trees
A short walk along the sand
Brought to horses and a meadow
We called it "Indian land"
Because the Salish people
Kept their horses there
Two miles south from our house, another wonder
There a small creek flowed

Across the beach into the ocean
In the fall, when tide and surf were high
Coho salmon would skitter across the beach
Into the lake to spawn

Lundy is gone
His house has fallen into disrepair, needs paint
The windows are covered with dirt and sea mist
Like cataracts
No matter
The ocean can no longer be seen through them
The Pink Flamingo Motel blocks the view
And now Lundy's parlor is illuminated all night
With garish pink from the neon sign
How ironic! There has never been a flamingo
On this cool and foggy northern coast
Until the one on the neon sign
And the plastic ones that they sell inside
Coastal pines used to drop their cones
Onto the gravel road in front of Lundy's

But now the only cones there now
Are stickly paper ones
That once held cotton candy
There have been no rabbits in our yard of years
The coho are gone like Lundy, too
Cascade Head has been purchased by a
conservancy, thank God!
The last of the Silverspots, now endangered, live there
But we can't see the headland anymore
Because a two-story rental house obstructs our view
Thanks to lack of zoning laws
Horses no longer run on he Indian land
Instead, video poker and roulette
Are played in the casino where the horses were
The meadow is an asphalt parking lot
And when it rains, oil and grease
Wash down onto the beach
And kill the mole crabs
That fed the pinkfin perch

That fed the bright-eyed, curious harbor seals
That would follow me, in the third set of waves,
As I ran along the beach
As for those eight towns and villages
They have conglomerated into a strip mall
Called "Lincoln City" by some
"Those Twenty Miserable Miles"
Lundy's ghost moves through the fog
Pondering the degradation and the change
Ah, Lundy, fortunate Lundy
No longer fixed in time and space
You are free to travel back to when
This was a fair and different place

CHAPTER 3

The Towns of Lincoln City

"A model of strip city grotesque."

Oregon Gov. Tom McCall

"Right now in Lincoln City, there's an upper class and a lower class; a working class that works for the tourists and an upper class that owns the property."

Kurt Mende, 1995

Highway 101's route, slightly realigned at different locations, has changed little through Lincoln County since the Sijota family farmed the land, property later becoming Salishan. A small pedestrian tunnel under the highway, now used by hundreds of golfers yearly at the Salishan golf course, was used by the Sijotas to move cattle from one side of the highway to the other. Emily Sijota had insisted on the tunnel when Highway 101 cut through her property. Farm buildings, residences and other remnants of early homesteaders are gone, replaced with the pampered greens and Scottish link motif of Salishan's renowned golf course.

The present highway presents a bleak picture of development and coastal sprawl, a sharp contrast to Salishan's understated elegance.

From the north, Highway 101 drops into Lincoln City after a steep north side Cascade Head ascent and south side descent, the southern side crossing the Salmon River estuary. The tourist from the north has probably visited the Tillamook cheese factory in Tillamook, a depressed city 45 miles north of Lincoln City, taken a brief Highway 101 detour to Three Capes Drive scenic route through Pacific City and seen the famous dory fleet, and pulled over at the Cascade Head lookout for a Pacific panorama including the Salmon River estuary, all part of the Cascade Head Scenic Research Area. Cascade Head was named for the cascading waters of several creeks and during World War II served as a Coast Guard lookout station.

Centered on the Oregon Coast and dead-center between the equator and North Pole at the 45th parallel, Lincoln City is an amalgamation of several towns and unincorporated areas, all consolidated by voters in 1964 after two failed efforts including one which lost by 7 votes in 1962. Oceanlake, named for the combination of the Pacific Ocean and Devils Lake, a 3-mile long lake in the center of town created as a result of a long ago blockage of a coastal stream and strangled in recent years by algae until grass carp were introduced, a move which managed to upset the lake's ecology even further; Cutler City, an unincorporated area named for the Cutler family who purchased the property from Charley DePoe, a Siletz Indian; Taft, named for President William Howard Taft; Delake, a name derived from the pronunciation of Devils Lake by the Finnish population; and Nelscott, a name formed by the combination of the town's developers, Charles P. Nelson and Dr. W.G. Scott;. three city names and two unincorporated names disappeared as voters on Dec. 8, 1964 combined the areas into Lincoln City, a bland name but one which solved the naming wars among the affected cities. It could have been "Surfland," the name pushed by local school children. But that name was too "honky-tonk" in the opinion of some.

VISUAL BLIGHT

Oregon Gov. Mark Hatfield was direct in his criticism of "junk" on the Oregon Coast. Speaking to a group in 1964, Hatfield called the consolidated towns "20 Miserable Miles," a jab at the Chamber of Commerce's "20 Miracle Miles."

Unfortunately the visual blight hasn't changed significantly in 40 years. Once Highway 101 enters Lincoln City the eyesores multiply, the entire picture further sullied by a ganglia of overhead power lines, some of which are finally being buried in northern and southern sections of the city. This stretch of Highway 101 offers the commercial ugliness of a miles-long strip mall as noted by Gov. Tom McCall who dubbed it "a model of strip city grotesque." A Pennsylvania college professor and noted ecological planner, Ian McHarg, called the city a "dismal specter" in 1970. The Taft area, on the south end of the strip, has recently spruced up and has significantly improved in appearance, the lone exception. The City is moving ahead with other "beautification" plans and there has been some progress.

Summer traffic snarls keep vacationers and local residents inching through the conglomeration of tourist bait. Views of the beach are limited, D River Wayside offering the easiest and most popular access. But recent years have seen the beach shadowed by enormous kites, creating the city's self-proclaimed "Kite Capital of the World" moniker.

D River Wayside adds another glimpse of Lincoln City's claim to fame; the world's shortest river. The concrete channel, a 440-foot long waterway, flows from a grate across Devils Lake to the sea, not exciting by itself but yet another attempt at luring tourists to an area for which tourism is a major industry, replacing the logging and fishing industries. Floating logs, remnants from the nearly defunct timber industry, often wash into low-level hotel rooms or onto the D River parking lot as winter storms push waves into seawalls with spectacular results.

Residents of Lincoln City talked for years of a Highway 101 bypass, a way around the dawdling RVs and Portland day-trippers. The early routing of Highway 101 through coastal towns such as Lincoln City and Coos Bay further south guaranteed the current traffic jams and conglomeration of tacky shops. The only bypass skirts Devils Lake but it saves little travel time. Merchants along 101 weren't anxious for a bypass and were lukewarm to any kind of divider on 101.

For those travelers willing to leave the security of Highway 101, the Road's End area offers more beach access in a spectacular setting. But in recent years a man-made diversion off Logan Road to Road's End hooked thousands of tourists and locals alike: Chinook Winds Casino. Build it and they will come. And come they did–by the thousands. Just turn at the fake lighthouse and you're almost there; a casino with an ocean view.

REEL 'EM IN

In recent years there were always rumors on the Coast about gambling. Employees at Salishan or other hotels such as the Hilton in Agate Beach "knew" that ballrooms had been pre-wired for slot machines. "Social gambling" including blackjack was permitted in some taverns. Bets were often substantial at places such as the Pip Tide in Newport, and the games danced around city ordinances permitting gambling. 2005 rumors circulated around plans to redesignate Siletz Bay so a floating casino could open for business.

"Did you hear about the latest Lincoln City white wine (whine)?" was the joke making the Lincoln City rounds in 1994. "Why can't we have a casino, why can't we have a casino?."

As the fourth Oregon tribe to enter into the casino business, the Confederated Tribes of the Siletz hadn't originally intended for the multi-million dollar casino to be sited overlooking the Pacific Ocean in Lincoln City. The tribe first wanted to build in the small Willamette Valley town of Donald but local politics scuttled that idea. Next was a 20-acre site in north Salem, but the Salem City council in 1992 rejected the idea as did Gov. Barbara Roberts. The tribe purchased the Salem land anyway but political opposition ("a casino in Salem would erode the social and moral fabric of the community and the quality of life would decline," said Gov. Roberts) sent the Tribe's interest to the Coast. In 1994 the 103rd U.S. Congress granted a request from the tribe to buy back 11 acres of oceanfront land, once part of the Siletz Reservation but sold in 1956, and place the land in trust, the same legal status as a reservation; a sovereign nation. The acreage was purchased from Shilo Inn owner Mark Hemstreet, part of his 80-acre oceanfront resort development. In 2004 Hemstreet, in financial trouble, also agreed to sell the Shilo Inn, an oceanfront motel next to the casino to the Tribe. An RV park is also in the planning stages by the Tribe. A 2005 sale saw the Lakeside Health and Fitness Club and golf course bought by the Tribe.

What went around came around. The casino site was originally part of the tribe's reservation, established in 1855. Under the Allotment Act of 1892 the original 80-acre oceanfront site went to a tribal member but was later sold to a private owner before being returned to the tribe in the Hemstreet sale. The site also coincidentally sits next to Hemstreet's other development, Lincoln Shores Star Resort, an upscale subdivision. Employees of the Shilo Inn and Lincoln Star were always quick to point out that the $44 million casino had no connection to other properties. In approving Lincoln Star in 1992 Lincoln City officials required development of a 200-seat convention center and/or hotel. Chinook Winds conveniently offered 20,000 square feet of meeting and convention space.

Officially opened in 1996 after a temporary location in a 10,000-square foot tent for more than a year, the 158,000-square foot casino immediately became Lincoln County's largest private employer with nearly 800 employees and a projected payroll of $10 million, wages above the minimum subsistence dollars of the fish and chips restaurants or candy-striped fudge shops. Median household income for the city, based on the 2000 census, is $24,959 while the per capita income for the city is $15,597. The dollars translate to 16.1% of the population below the poverty line and 12.5% of families in the same boat. Tourism jobs barely pay the bills. Casino jobs came a little closer to paying the rent if smoke-filled rooms and the depressing spectacle of money being poured into the slots 24-hours a day could be overlooked.

Originally managed in part by Comstock Hotel/Casino in Reno, Nev., with a 30 percent net to Comstock and 70 percent to the Tribe on a five-year contract, the coastal casino opened with great fanfare in June 1996, accompanied by citizen concern in Lincoln City and a gnawing feeling that the casino project had been shoved down their collective throats. There were few public hearings on the project. An opposition group, the No Casino Association, had little impact although organizers claimed 1,400 members. The tribe's property was a separate nation and not subject to zoning laws. The tribe could contract with local fire and police departments. As an example, in 2005 the tribe agreed to pay Lincoln County $85,000 for county services. An agreement in 2005 with Lincoln City gave the City $350,000 per year to replace lost transient room revenues after the Shilo Inn was sold to the Tribe.

The expected tourist dollar increase for local businesses never materialized as the fish were reeled into the casino. As one local businesswoman noted, "...when you insert casino gambling into a tourist economy, you have no net increase in dollars. You simply have a shift of dollars from retail businesses and restaurants to the casino."

A 1999 economic impact study substantiated that opinion, noting that $4.8 million, mostly in food and beverage, was the "direct substitution effect," dollars spent at the casino instead of local businesses. The report also noted that those local losses were more than offset by $14.8 in spending elsewhere in the area by tourists lured by the casino. Motel room night sales increased and more rooms were built including chains such as Motel 6. Highway 101 traffic, already snarled, increased by 10 percent as a result of the casino.

Home Box Office (HBO) prizefights ("Commotion at the Ocean"), B-list entertainers, piped in music flooding the parking lots, searchlights and the promise of jackpots from the more than 800 slot machines kept the bleary-eyed nickel-and-dime rollers tethered to their slots with the casino card on a rope, a way to track just about every gambling move. Blackjack tables lured those with a few more dollars and later years saw craps, more slots, keno and other full-scale casino games transform the oceanfront setting into to a Las Vegas-style operation.

The fish came through town, tried to beat the unbeatable house odds while sucking in smoke-filled air, lost a few hundred, ate a gut-busting buffet and occasionally glanced outside at a Pacific sunset or, more likely, a Coast Range sunrise. Brought in by the busloads and often staying within walking distance at the Shilo, the mostly over 50 crowd rarely ventured outside the smoke-shrouded banks of slots, transfixed instead by the flashing neon and gimmicks. No coins at the slots. Insert a dollar or a $5 or a $10, $20 or $100 and the credits magically appeared on the slot screen. No noisy coin payouts, just paper payout slips, assuming there was a payoff.

When the bus was ready for the return trip to Portland and it was check-out time at the Shilo, reality set in as the weary gamblers trudged outside and boarded the bus. In town the new pawnshops opened for business.

TRAVEL TO THE COAST

Traveling to Lincoln City and Salishan can be an adventure, a fact the 1996 corporate buyers of Salishan Lodge failed to recognize. A 2005 survey from the American Highway Users Alliance named Highways 18, 20 and 22 to the Oregon Coast as number one in the United States in terms of the highest levels of delays caused by traffic bottlenecks. Air travel isn't much of an option. Siletz Bay airport (adjacent to Salishan Lodge) is limited to small planes. Commuter air service in Newport, 25 miles south, was tried but failed on numerous occasions. Some drivers choose Oregon Highway 20 between Corvallis and Newport, a winding highway subject to the popular bumper sticker "Pray for Me, I Drive Highway 20." Chip trucks, making their way to and from the Georgia-Pacific mill in Toledo, cram the two-lane road. Once reaching Newport, the tourist could travel north on Highway 101 through the seemingly never-ending maintenance work along a poorly designed section paralleling Beverly Beach; across Cape Foulweather where 150-feet of the roadway dropped 80-feet down a cliff in December 1999 and left the main connecting route between Newport and Lincoln City with a giant gap; or take the old highway past the ever-struggling Inn at Otter Crest. Once over the Foulweather grade, the highway drops into Depoe Bay, another conglomeration of tourist bait and ocean spray. A few miles north Salishan Lodge nestles into the hillside.

Visitors to Lincoln City and later Salishan usually drove via Oregon Highway 18 through "The Corridor." Highway 18 was completed in 1930 and took visitors from Salem through Grand Ronde and into a Douglas-fir tunnel known as the VanDuzer Forest Corridor. The two-lane highway, originally a toll road, was named for Henry VanDuzer, a Portland civic leader and long-time state highway commission chairman. Van Duzer, president of Inman Poulsen Lumber Company at the time of his death in 1951, was Portland's first citizen in 1939, and was compared with Portland leaders such as Simon Benson, John Yeon and Robert Booth.

The one-hour drive from Salem, often a two-hour return on Sunday nights, passes by another Oregon landmark, one which has surpassed Multnomah Falls as Oregon's leading tourist attraction; Spirit Mountain Casino, another Native American casino and one which dwarfs Chinook Winds. Without a stop at Spirit Mountain (or in earlier years a stop for strawberry shortcake or a carton of fresh eggs from the roadside stand with an honor system of paying), the trip from Portland takes 2 hours and crosses scenic coastal steams such as Widow's Creek, Bear Creek and Slick Rock Creek, so named for the mossy covered rocks which made horse crossings a chancy endeavor. Snow in the winter is a possibility and the 1,000 foot summits often receive a few inches of heavy, damp flakes. Returning to Portland on Sunday nights could take 3 or 4 hours as the towns of Dundee and Newberg crunch the homeward bound into narrow streets with stoplights and well-known speed traps.

Salishan employees later would try and explain to the new

corporate owners that a business conference center on the Oregon Coast wasn't a feasible plan given the transportation issues. But the plan moved ahead anyway and was a failure.

Highway 18 merges smoothly onto Highway 101, the intersection directing travelers north to the trendy beach cottage village of Neskowin and, further north, Tillamook, while the south route funnels traffic in to the northern city limits of Lincoln City.

Let the billboards begin.

Once past the casino turnout the traveler is again met with tourist businesses and franchises. Quality restaurants are scarce, a fact noted by John Storrs in later years when he called Lincoln City a "gastronomical dustbowl," a candid but routine comment from the Salishan Lodge architect. Interestingly, the one restaurant standout in later years would be Blackfish, a restaurant owned by former Salishan chef Rob Pounding.

A factory outlet mall on the Highway 101 east side offers architecturally dull sprawl with the usual staples such as Levis, Eddie Bauer and Maidenform. The mall brought in busloads of tourists in pre-casino days, but competition in the Willamette Valley reduced the outlet's popularity.

Continue south for another 8 miles and a stoplight, the last one before Newport 25 miles south, is triggered by traffic exiting Salishan Lodge on the left, "THE Resort on the Oregon Coast" as proclaimed by the original wooden carved sign, or the Marketplace shopping center to the east.

Past the stoplight and on the west side of Highway 101 is the golf pro shop. A right turn, up a small incline and through the Salishan gate. Beyond the gate is a world of sand dunes, architectural committees and the Pacific Ocean.

CHAPTER 4

Buying the Land

"We saw them (the Indians) now and then but we didn't have any truck with them."

Emily Sijota

Named for the U.S. President after a debate between the names Bay County and Blaine County, Lincoln County was formed in 1893 and encompassed parts of Benton and Polk counties. With an area of 1,009 square miles, Lincoln County stretches from south of Yachats to north of Lincoln City and into the Coast Range. The current county seat is Newport, the end of the road in the early 1900s as transportation north and south was limited, mostly wagon trials and beaches. Trains brought the tourists to the Coast from the Willamette Valley. But a coastal highway was needed.

Several events converged to make construction of a coastal highway a reality. World War I and Henry Ford's development of the automobile paved the way for the Oregon legislature to pass the nation's first gasoline tax in 1919. Enter Ben Jones, variously described as a steamboat captain, lawyer, mayor of both Newport and Toledo, developer, and "Father of Lincoln County," a reference to Jones' leadership in splitting Lincoln County away from Benton and Polk Counties. But it was Jones's introduction of a bill in the Oregon House of Representatives that sealed his legacy. His legislation authorized Oregon bonding authority of $2.5 million for highway construction. Named the Roosevelt Coast Military Highway, a name sure to attract federal dollars which eventually came, the proposed highway stretched from the Columbia River on the north to the California state line on the south, more than 300 miles of roadway and spectacular bridges designed by state highway engineer Conde McCullough. By 1923 construction had begun. Jones' reward was the naming of bridge for him in Otter Rock, a village south of Lincoln City which Jones had bought and platted earlier

Highway 101 became the main highway, replacing the El Camino Real, Olympic Highway and Pacific Highway signage with the easily recognizable Highway 101 shield. A bridge across the Siletz River completed in 1926 eliminated the need for a ferry.

TRUST PATENTS

The 80-acre "trust patents," issued to Indians instead of deeds with future sales restricted without government authorization, covered much of the property destined for Salishan, especially the west side of Highway 101. The five major landowners were granted the property from the U.S Government in 1894, authorized by the Dawes Act of 1887;

Alsea Johnson-Johnson's property was 79.75 acres and included lots 3,4 and 5 in section 3, property west of the current Highway 101. Johnson sold the property in 1908 to Charles Henry and George Dekum, sold again to Lulu Lankford in 1923 with the death of Charles Henry; again in 1944 as Lankford sold the land to J.R. Haight and Floy Haight. The death of J.R. Haight resulted in the sale of the nearly 80 acres to Lyle and Gladys Hasselbrink in 1953.

Edward Wilson-Wilson's 80 acres went to Albert Sijota in 1908 although it's not clear from court records if Sijota bought the property or it was granted to him, possibly as a result of Wilson's death. Albert sold one of the parcels back to his brother Joseph in 1912, Joseph to his daughter Valentine in 1915, the rest of Albert's property sold in 1935 to C.R. Thorpe. Thorpe sold the land in 1945 to J.R. Haight and Floy Haight, and again in 1953 as Lyle Hasselbrink and Gladys Hasselbrink increased their beachfront holdings.

Lucy Wilson-this small 15- acre parcel also ended up with the Hasselbrinks in 1953.

George Stanton and Ollie Stanton-a large parcel of 122 acres was sold to Joseph Sijota in 1905, and stayed in the Sijota family.

THE SIJOTAS

Joseph Sijota may have seen the government newspaper

advertisements for the Oregon coastal land or word of mouth may have made it back to Wisconsin where Joseph, his family and his brothers lived a middle class lifestyle. But migration fever and a chance to own more land was sweeping through the United States. Joseph Sijota had immigrated from Austria to Wisconsin in 1879 where he met his future wife, Mary.

The brothers—Joseph, Mike, John, Albert and their father Walenty-- came west, exploring Oregon as far south as Medford before settling on the Siletz Bay area. In 1905 Joseph Sijota bought the George Stanton parcel of 122 acres and a year later was granted 39 acres by the U.S. Government.

The Sijota families, including Joseph and Mary with their 9 children, were now Oregonians. Four more children would be born to Joseph and Mary.

The entire area was known as Sijota, a name later changed to Gleneden Beach with the purchase of some of the land by the Cary family from Joseph Fogarty and named after one of their daughters-- plus the advertising gimmick of "eden" added to assist in future land sales. The town was dedicated in 1927, a time when one of the Joseph and Mary Sijota's daughters, Emily, was postmistress. Later efforts in the 1970s to incorporate Gleneden Beach and the Salishan properties would fail.

On the Siletz River the fish cannery was in full operation in the early 1900s and on the south side of the river a sawmill would encourage a small settlement known as Millport.

Emily Sijota described her early life on the coastal property including references to Indians living on the end of the sand spit "where trees don't grow. We saw them (the Indians) now and then but we didn't have any truck with them."

The Sijotas farmed the land, hunted ducks on Siletz Bay, were successful trappers and raised dairy cattle. In one remembrance, and one which would have ramifications many years later, Emily Sijota recalled a time when a wave washed over the spit and into the bay.

Glass floats, now collector's items, routinely washed up on the Siletz Spit beach where Emily and her sisters would just as routinely smash them to bits.

Emily Sijota eventually ended up with the majority of land ownership, 116 acres, and was postmistress at the Gleneden Beach post office beginning in 1929. She died in 1986.

The Sijota and Hasselbrink lands were key to Salishan development as the property included some ocean frontage and land where the current west side golf course is located.

But developer John Gray's initial goal, along with those of his partners in the late 1950s, was development in Portland in an area later known as Mountain Park, a hilly property on the east side of Interstate 5 and south of the Portland city limits in Lake Oswego, an upscale housing destination for Portlanders. Gray picked his associates carefully.

Russell Colwell was a native Portlander, born in "The Rose City" on January 1, 1900. He attended Lincoln High School and joined the Army in 1917. He returned home after a 2-1/2 year stint and attended Oregon State University, graduating with a 4-year degree, and immediately began work as a bond teller in the Portland-based Security Savings and Trust Bank. He later became assistant cashier and, in 1928, First National Bank bought Security Savings. Colwell was promoted to vice president in 1931 and senior vice-president in 1960.

Colwell headed up the municipal bond department and, by his estimate, would trade more than $100 billion in bonds during his 42-year career including Panama Canal bonds. Colwell's civic involvement in Portland included trustee of Willamette University (Salem), president of Oregon Motor Association, member of the Portland Development Commission, as well as numerous other civic involvements.

It was Colwell's personal trading in U.S. government treasury bonds which gave him his investment funds for Salishan and other developments.

Gray described Colwell as "enthusiastic;" "always very cheerful type person, nice to work with."

Paul Hebb was born Sept. 27, 1904, in the Canadian Yukon Territory and graduated from the University of Washington and Stanford University. He worked for Dean Witter & Co. in Tacoma Wa., before moving to Portland in 1948 and was the owner of Safway Scaffolding Company and later the Country Store, a department store in Lake Oswego. Hebb was also the developer of numerous business properties in Beaverton along with his wife Marion (who died in 1958), served on the Oregon Economic Development Commission, and was also a member of the Lewis and Clark College board of directors. Active in Republican circles, Hebb coordinated fundraising projects for Mark Hatfield and Bob Packwood.

"Paul (Hebb) was more practical on the nuts and bolts of the infrastructure, how to get things done on the ground," Gray said.

Donald G. Drake was a short-time partner and his family would later develop Mt. Hood Meadows, a ski resort on the slopes of Mt. Hood. John Gray served as one of the first directors.

The partners couldn't reach an agreement with the Platt family for the Mountain Park purchase and began to look elsewhere for development possibilities including visits to property near Siletz Bay, an area well-known by Gray. John and his wife, Betty Gray, owned a small beach house in Lincoln City and John Gray recalls hiking on property which he would later buy and develop into Salishan, the first planned unit development in Oregon. A coincidental golf meeting set the stage for the first property purchase.

SALISHAN-$420 PER ACRE

Lyle Hasselbrink was a native Oregonian. Born in 1910 in Wilsonville, Ore., Hasselbrink owned the Oceanlake Sand and Gravel Company in Lincoln City from 1939 to 1965 and was actively involved in local organizations. He served on the Port of Newport as chairman and on the North Lincoln Fire District. As the community of Oceanlake incorporated in 1945, Hasselbrink was on the first city council.

By 1960 Lyle and his wife, Gladys, had accumulated approximately 165 acres of land north of the Sijota dairy farm and onto Siletz Spit to the current guest parking lot. Gray would meet Hasselbrink by chance in Indio, Ca., where Gray had gone for spring vacation and a few rounds of golf, a Gray passion. In one of those rounds Gray ended up in the same golf foursome with Hasslebrink, found out it was the same person who owned the property, and the two discussed the possibility of a sale. Hasselbrink returned to Oceanlake, listed the land with real estate agent Edward Eaton of Beach Properties Inc. and Eaton sent a letter to Gray offering the property.

On July 19, 1961, wheels were set in motion for Salishan as Gray and his partners entered a 5-year purchase agreement for the

Hasselbrink property north of the Sijota farm for $48,000, terms of $13,920 down and equal payments for $8,520 per year for four years. Also in 1961 a small parcel was purchased from Donn DeBernardi for $12,500 which included the tip of the spit to the present common park area. In previous years fireworks were launched from the tip of the spit as part of the city's Fourth of July celebration. DeBernardi recalled the sale.

"They (the developers) came driving down in a big, brand new Lincoln and parked in front of my real estate office" DeBernardi said in a 2005 interview. DeBernardi had purchased the property two years earlier from Lyle Hasselbrink and Loyd Calkins for $5,000 and the easiest access was by boat.

The property purchases were acquired in quarter interests by each partner although Drake dropped out in 1962, leaving Gray and Colwell with 3/8ths interest each and Hebb 1/4 interest. Colwell and Gray bought out Hebb's interest in 1964 and, in 1975, Gray purchased Colwell's 50 percent interest for $100,000 spread out over 5 years. Paul Hebb died in 1989, Russell Colwell died in 1986

Although the Hasselbrink purchase was a key purchase, the major land purchase came a few months later as the Emily Sijota and Frank Sijota lands came into the partnership ownership. Emily Sijota's 116 acres sold for $80,000, the Frank Sijota property for $22,500, an additional 35 acres.

Gray individually purchased additional acreage in 1962 on the east side of Highway 101. This included 195 acres from George and Clara Kirkpatrick, W.W. and Meta Kirkpatrick, and Alice and Archie Passmore; 6 acres from Frank Jones. Salishan Lodge would be built on 12 acres from the Kirkpatrick sale, the remainder would be developed as Salishan Hills. Gray also negotiated a deal with Longview Fiber which owned acreage along the future second nine holes. In order to arrange the purchase Gray first had to purchase 100 acres of timberland on the Siletz River owned by Christ Church, the Benjamin Dagwell Foundation and the Medical Research Foundation. That land was then traded to Longview Fiber for the 43 acres Gray wanted for Salishan and phase two of Salishan Hills.

Title for the westside land was briefly in the partner's names until a corporation was formed in early January 1962: Salishan Properties Inc. The corporation assumed annual payments on the contracts while the partners paid the pro-rata portions on land still individually owned.

Everything was in place for the Salishan development to proceed. With 320 acres on the Spit and an additional 200 acres on the east side of the highway, the partners had two miles of ocean frontage and two miles of bay frontage. On the Spit were spruce, coast pine, hemlock, salal, huckleberry, rhododendron, kinnikinnick and Indian paintbrush. Average price paid per acre: $420.

The Salishan Spit was ready for a makeover.

While the developers were quietly purchasing the Salishan property, life to the north in the small coastal towns of Oceanlake, Cutler City and others on the ocean's shore moved quietly–and sometimes not so quietly. Devils Lake Yacht Club had its first meeting in the clubhouse, a police officer was fired, Sea Horse motel opened for business, weeds in Devil's Lake created problems for boats and water skiers and 66 seniors graduated from Taft High School.

On the Siletz Spit, 9 miles south of Taft, things were about to change dramatically.

CHAPTER 5

John and Betty Gray

"Gray's entry into large scale land development is a calculated attempt to raise Oregon's backwoodsy taste to a level in keeping with its natural beauty. His concept couldn't have come along at a better time for Oregon, on the eve of mass discovery by trampled Californians wending their way northward."

Sports Illustrated, April 1969

Greatest Business Leader: John Gray
Best Hotel or Motel; Salishan Lodge
Best Resort: Sunriver

"The Best of Oregon", Ken Metzler, 1986

Oregon entered the 1960s perched on the edge of dramatic growth. John Gray's timing was ideal, but it was a vision of how his developments fit into the environment that became his legacy.

John Dalton Gray was born to Mabel R. and R. Elmer Gray on July 29, 1919, in Ontario, Oregon, an Eastern Oregon agricultural community within a Snake River boat ride to Idaho and a one-hour freeway drive to Boise.

John Gray's father, a rancher, suffered rheumatic fever as a child, weakening his heart and eventually resulting in a fatal heart attack when John Gray was 6 years old. Mother and sons moved to Corvallis where Mabel Gray's parents lived and the young widow returned to Oregon State University for additional certifications for teaching, a profession she practiced until her marriage. She would teach in a one-room schoolhouse in a rural farm area three miles north of the small town of Monroe where John Gray and his two younger brothers attended her classes.

John Gray graduated from Oregon State University with a degree in secretarial science (business), spent five and one-half years in the Army during World War II in the European theater, and returned home as a lieutenant colonel with a Bronze Star to attend Harvard Business School, earning a master's degree. Gray was accepted at both Stanford and Harvard but chose Harvard with his G.I. Bill benefits because the university offered a shorter program.

Gray carried his love of learning into the business world. Asked in 1972 why he was obsessed with quality, Gray said:

"Just a continual awareness that you do things, you can have things, you can be around things, irregardless of your income level, that makes life more pleasant. And that generally leads to excellence. I guess I've always insisted on that. In the academic areas I was a top student. Maybe that's where it started because I loved to learn and find out about more things"

THE BEETLE SOLUTION

Gray returned to Oregon in 1947 and went to work briefly for Pointer Williamette, a company manufacturing logging and highway trailers. An acquaintance and Harvard business school classmate, Carter Stanley, encouraged Gray to join him at a fledging company in Portland called Oregon Saw Manufacturing. Gray made the move in 1948.

The Oregon Saw Manufacturing was founded in 1947 with four employees and one product, a new type of chain for gas-powered chainsaws. Logging was the major industry in Oregon and an easier way to cut the giant Douglas Firs and Sitka Spruce was needed.

In 1946 a timber beetle, being watched intently by Joseph Cox, was easily munching its way through a piece of tree stump. That beetle would provide the answer to a question pondered by Cox, a logger, who used chainsaws regularly but spent most of his time filing and maintaining the troublesome chain.

"I spent several months looking for nature's answer to the problem," Cox recalled in an interview for a company newsletter. "I found it in the...timber beetle."

Cox observed the C-shape alternating jaws of the beetle which could chew through timber both across and with the wood grain.

Duplicating the design in steel and working out of his home on NE 33rd Ave. in Portland, Cox sold his first Cox Chipper Chain in 1947 and, at the time and even today, the design is considered one of the biggest influences in timber harvesting. Within seven years Oregon Saw Manufacturing Company had become the world's largest manufacturer of cutting chains for the chain saw.

Oregon wasn't the only market for Cox's innovative chain. By 1955 nearly 75 percent of the chains went to markets east of the Mississippi.

Joining the company in 1948, John Gray was hired as the company's sixteenth employee at the same time the company was moving into larger Portland facilities. Gray was 28 at the time and reports from the period noted the fact that Gray's first chair at the company was a empty nail keg.

"I liked the challenge of being in on the ground floor of something so exciting with so much obvious potential," Gray said.

Four years later sales topped $1 million and the company went multinational, purchasing the Planer Chain Ltd. of Guleph, Ontario, Canada.

In 1953 the Oregon Saw Chain Company was sold to Gray. Gray paid Cox $5,000 cash plus numerous notes and 15 percent of sales the first five years and 10 percent the following 10 years. Gray said he saw a potential for the company, "an interesting opportunity."

"I envisioned a lot of growth for it (the company)," Gray said. "We had to develop the markets."

John D. Gray in 1972.
Oregonian newspaper.

By 1955 the company had more than 200 employees. Cox died Aug. 10, 2002, in Santa Barbara, Ca. He was 97.

While the cutting chain business was the backbone of the company, accounting for more than 51 percent of sales in 1955, Gray was ready for expansion. The acquisitions would include companies involved in construction, fastening tools, a timber harvesting company, and ammunition. A classmate of Gray's at Harvard was Ed Cooley and Gray hired Cooley as assistant general manager of Oregon Saw Manufacturing. A separate company, Precision Castparts, was formed as a subsidiary in 1953 and Cooley bought the company in 1957. Precision Castparts would become a leading international aircraft parts manufacturer and Cooley would become a multi-millionaire and a major philanthropic and business leader in Oregon including ownership of Hillsboro Aviation. He and John Gray would meet on the Salishan Spit in later years as the Spit developed and Cooley served on the Salishan homeowners board of directors.

Oregon Saw Manufacturing Company's name was changed to Omark Industries in 1956, a combination of Oregon and trademark. Gray noted the Omark name also translated well in foreign languages.

OMARK

Omark was homegrown, a true Oregon company which sprang from the innovative genius of Joseph Cox but prospered under John Gray's ownership. The scope of Gray's work became clear in 1964 as Omark Industries Inc. went public with an offering of 550,000 shares of stock. Similar to Tektronix which was privately held by two men, Gray and his family had been the owners of Omark during the meteoric profit rise. A prospectus for the stock sale showed Gray owned 1,083,520 shares of common stock, Elizabeth (Betty) Gray owned 200,000 shares and a trust for his children owned 50,000 shares. Omark was authorized to issue 4 million shares without par value and there were 2,005,000 shares outstanding. Income per share in 1964 showed each share earned $1.24 for the year ending in June.

The sale prospectus, filed with the Securities and Exchange Commission, noted the stock would come from Gray's holdings with 228,170 from Gray himself, none from Elizabeth Gray and 20,000 shares from the children's trust. True to Gray's later departing cash gift to employees of Salishan Lodge, Gray set 20,000 shares aside for sale to Omark employees.

The sale of stock forced Omark to reveal sales and profit figures and they were staggering. Sales were $10,460,000 in 1960, $11,800,000 in 1961, $15,231,000 in 1962, $18,000,000 in 1963 and nearly $23 million in 1964.

By 1964 Omark's sales were 70 percent from the saw chains and related products, 20 percent from fastening equipment, 5 percent from welding equipment and 5 percent from industrial diamond products.

Gray also set the company apart in another aspect; unions. By 1964 Omark had 1,200 employees with approximately 900 in the United States, 250 in Canada and 50 in the rest of the world. There was no union representation nor would there be any at future Gray developments.

"We tried to create an atmosphere where unions wouldn't do the employees any good," Gray recalled. "We felt we did the right thing. We had profit sharing. We made a good effort to provide excellent employment opportunities and working conditions."

Omark Industries became part of the New York Stock Exchange in 1967 as sales projections reached the $45 million mark.

Seventeen years later, November 26, 1984, the Omark stock sales were halted on the Exchange as rumors circulated regarding the possible sale of Omark. The rumors proved true. Blount Inc., a Montgomery, Ala.-based company, was the buyer for $268 million. Internationally recognized in construction and engineering, Blount had projected sales in 1985 of $819 million with 6,000 permanent employees. Omark sales in 1984 were $297 million.

The sale gave stockholders of Omark $37.50 per share (book value of Omark stock in the previous year was listed at $20.75), plus additional compensation to current executives of Omark.

Blount acquired 42.6 percent of the shares including Gray's 1.4 million shares and Elizabeth Gray's 535,532 shares, 28% of the total shares. The Grays came out of the deal with $74 million.

In commenting at the time on the sale, Gray said Blount was the first corporate inquiry that Omark took seriously after several years of numerous offers from other companies. Blount executives became aware of Omark after a visit to Japan. According to reports, Blount was interested in acquiring companies which practiced "Japanese methods" in the manufacturing processes. Winton Blount said his company was interested in diversification and were tipped to the Omark style while in Japan. A meeting with Gray and a merger agreement was reached, but only after offering Gray nearly twice the value of his stock.

Omark was Blount's first excursion into the Portland market.

Gray in his usual modest manner, said after the stockholders approved the merger with Blount that "the shareholders provided the equity and the employees provided the man-hours and hours of work."

Gray said he took pride in the merger and that he and his wife "had a hand in determining what the new ownership would be."

Gray retired several months after the merger, announcing his retirement by saying "change has to happen. I'm not going to stay on this earth forever."

Gray said the Omark sale "solves the problem of my own estate" and he wanted to be able to make sure the transition was handled well. At the time Gray was also chairman of the board at Tektronix and other board memberships including Standard Insurance.

Reflecting on his Omark employment, Gray noted, again in a 1972 interview, about quality.

"The consistency is the desire for quality in whatever I do, whether it's in Omark, where we try to insist on quality in people, products, plants, ways of doing business, our land development, or something else. The same way with art and craft work. I get an enjoyment out of being associated with a good work of art or good pieces of craft work, good carpenter work or good landscaping."

He would later comment that "quality pays off in the long run.""It's how you live your own life," he said. "It should have a lot of quality in it. I think people, in general, like quality, respect quality and enjoy quality."

The Omark name would disappear in 1989 as Blount Inc. consolidated divisions.

PUBLIC SERVICE

A Portland contractor, commenting on John Gray, noted that "no one has made a more consistently bold statement as to what the quality of development in Oregon should be."

In a 1973 address to the National Association of Homeowners Gray noted that Oregon has "the toughest environmental laws of all 50 states and yet Oregon economy exceeds the national average."

"I am unalterably convinced that for the land developer, ecological consideration is another way of spelling expanded opportunity, that the more intelligent the land use, the more the profit potential," Gray said.

The idea that a land developer might be sensitive to land use considerations and the ecology was a radical concept in the 1960s as Oregon headed down the road of helter-skelter developments.

"I had a strong in interest in more controlled development instead of sprawl,' Gray said.

Oregon land use development was coming under scrutiny and, in 1973, Gov. Tom McCall made his now famous speech to the state legislature in which he characterized "coastal condomania" and "sagebrush subdivisions" in Oregon as an "unfettered despoiling of the land." Gray knew McCall.

"He (McCall) was very positive. He had ideas and expressed them well. He got a lot of things done," Gray said.

Although the Oregon legislature had passed Senate Bill 10 in 1969 which required every city and county in the state to have a comprehensive land use plan meeting state goals and standards, the teeth were missing to enforce the law or provide assistance from the state. And so cities and counties simply ignored the law.

The McCall speech, accompanied by lobbying throughout the state, led to the passage of Senate Bill 100 in 1973 creating the Land Conservation and Development Commission (LCDC), a bill signed by McCall.

Senate Bill 100 created statewide protections for farmland. LCDC's first major task was to adopt 14 statewide planning goals to govern local land use plans. Later amendments included four "goals" to protect coastal resources. Several attempts at overturning the state legislation failed.

Throughout the process, John Gray was an active proponent of intelligent land-use planning.

"Oregonians are convinced LCDC is a valuable part of keeping Oregon a livable state. State-approved local plans provide...much greater certainty to the new businesses and developers who must meet land-use requirements,." Gray said in 1994. Henry Richmond, instrumental in formation of 1000 Friends of Oregon, recalls Gray's involvement.

"Gray was one of the few prominent members of the business community to testify on behalf of Senate Bill 100 in 1973."

In 1982 efforts to gut the state's land-use laws via Ballot Measure 6 were defeated and the main financial backer in the defeat was John Gray. In 2004 Oregon voters approved Measure 37, a measure many saw as the breakdown of Oregon's nationally recognized land-use laws. Gray, along with groups such as the

Nature Conservancy, donated $100,000 to defeat the measure, but the mood in Oregon had apparently changed. In 2005, however, a judge overturned the voter mandate, but an Oregon Supreme Court ruling in 2006 upheld the vote.

Gray was a whirlwind in Portland business circles during the 1960s and 1970s while, at the same time, developing the Salishan property. Named Portland's First Citizen of the Year in 1968, Gray's numerous civic service were noted including serving on the Reed College Board of Trustees for a remarkable 45 years where he raised millions of dollars for the college; member of the Board of Trustees for the Oregon Graduate Center, director and past president of the Portland Area Council of the Boy Scouts of America (Gray would personally purchase land for the Boy Scouts to use), and trustee of the Committee for Economic Development as well as the Portland Chamber of Commerce. And the list continued; chairman of the Riverdale School District; director, Portland Chamber of Commerce; director of First National Bank of Oregon, Standard Insurance, chairman of Tekronix, and director of Precision Castparts.

BETTY GRAY

John Gray met Elizabeth (Betty) Neuner, daughter of an Oregon attorney general, at Oregon State University and in 1946 the couple married in McMinnville, Oregon. The couple had five children; 4 daughters–Anne, Joan, Janet, Laurie-- and a son, Jack. One of the daughters, Anne Walrod, died suddenly in 1996 from a viral heart infection and her son, 25-year Nathan, was killed in a 2002 Mexican motorcycle accident. John and Betty Gray have 13 grandchildren and a great grandchild.

Betty Gray.
Photo courtesy of
Gray family.

Betty Gray was a force in Portland's philanthropic scene during the 1960s and early 1970s, volunteering for numerous committees and organizations, raising (and donating) millions of dollars for a variety of institutions including the Oregon Historical Society, Oregon Symphony, Reed College, Oregon Independent College Foundation, Cooperative Nursery School Council, Portland Junior Symphony and serving on dozens of other boards and councils. She was very active with the Oregon Health Sciences University (OHSU) and Loaves and Fishes.

Receiving a B.S. degree in Home Economics from Oregon State University and a Master's Degree in Student Personnel and Counseling from Columbia University, New York, Betty Gray served as Dean of Students at Corvallis High School prior to her marriage to John. She had taught school in West Linn, Oregon, and Grant High School in Portland. She was an accomplished pianist.

Betty Gray commented in the Catlin-Gabel School newsletter in 1971, comments which ring even more true today given the situation in Oregon schools.

"This is a difficult time for education in general, as many people are taking their frustrations out on the schools," she said. Grays' children attended the Portland private school and Betty Gray said she felt the upscale school gave the children three gifts not available in other schools."First, and most important, is a belief in the dignity of every person. Second, a love of learning. Finally, a respect for other viewpoints."

Betty Gray was described by Oregonian columnist Gerry Frank as "...one of the most effective community workers around." In the same column, Frank describes John Gray as "an extremely generous and environmentally conscious individual."

Betty Gray died of lung cancer April 10, 2003, at the age of 81. At a memorial concert on June 25, 2002, more than 300 people gathered at Reed College's Kaul Auditorium as the Chamber Music Northwest, still another recipient of John and Betty Gray's largesse, played selections from Bach, Schumann and Mozart. At a reception ice cream, a Betty Gray favorite, was served as students from the Community Music Center played. The Community Music Center in Portland, operated by the City of Portland, also received a grant from the Grays for new music rooms as well as future grants from her living trust.

"We donated most of the building (Community Music Center) after I convinced Ivancie (former Portland Mayor Frank Ivancie) that the council sign an agreement that they not change the purpose of the building for 10 or 15 years," Gray said in describing the City of Portland building. "I didn't want to spend money on remodeling, then have them (the council) change their mind on the purpose of the building."

Music played on the lawn of Reed College in front of the Gray Commons, the name a recognition of the multi-thousands of dollars donated by the Grays to the southeast Portland college.

"Again, it relates back to quality," Gray said in describing his donations to Reed. "I always wanted to be associated with an institute of higher education that demands quality and I saw it there."

"It was part of her (Betty Gray's) belief about what wealth was for–that it was about giving it away and doing good rather than piling it up," said Charles Allis, a long-time friend of the Grays.

The Grays were strong supporters of Northwest arts and it was Betty Gray who would incorporate much of the Northwest art still seen at Salishan Lodge today. In 2005 John Gray donated 40 Native American art objects to the Portland Art Museum, a donation valued in excess of $500,000. The Grays had been collecting the artwork since the 1970s and received the Governor's Art Award in 1983 as arts patrons. Betty Gray was also the Salishan Lodge "conscience," always on the alert for inappropriate signs or activities which didn't meet the Salishan standards of excellence.

GRAY'S LEGACY

While the Grays were certainly well-known in Portland, John Gray was always ill at ease in the public eye, preferring to stay in the background. Gray noted in 1972 that had he been doing the same thing in Los Angeles, nobody would notice.

"I don't like being visible," he said. Gray said he would prefer to let his actions and accomplishments speak for themselves. For example, those accomplishments have resulted in numerous philanthropic gifts such as more than $2 million to the Oregon Symphony.

A 1996 Oregonian article describing the sale of Salishan Lodge best described Gray.

"He's the one person in this state that I hold in the highest regard," said Robert Ames, former First Interstate Bank of Oregon president. "Oregon would be one very different place if not for John Gray."

Writer Steve Mayes, who wrote the Gray article, said "...those who watched Oregon grow the past 50 years don't refer to Gray as a developer. They call him a treasure, a pioneer, an idealist, and a philanthropist whose business ventures brought him wealth that he shared."

Gray, succinct as usual, said "...you do your share of public things, you do your share and maybe a little more if you can. If you have the money to give, fine. If you don't, devote the time."

A longtime friend of the Grays said "I'll bet John Gray has given more of his own money to charity than anybody else in Oregon, ever. And no one may ever know how much as many of the gifts were given anonymously."

Jonathan Nicolas, a well-known Portland columnist, noted how Gray stood out among the developers: "being a land developer in a way that shames 95 percent of those in the profession; being humble in a way that shames all those spotlight-seekers who scramble for acclaim; being a towering figure as he walks the Oregon stage. Through the last 30 years, Gray has almost single-handedly done more for tourism in Oregon than all the slogans combined,"

Nicholas said. "And the facilities he has created have been ones in harmony with this place."

Gray was one of the first to recognize Portland's Pearl District, now a thriving residential district. His Irving Street Lofts were built in 1989. Other Gray developments included Carmen Oaks, a care center for senior citizens, as well as assisted living centers in Tillamook, Hines and Lake Oswego built in the mid-1990s.

As one associate noted in 1982; "He (Gray) is a very humble guy and the first time you meet him it's hard to believe he's accomplished all he has."

One Reed College alumnus recognized Gray's contributions to the college.

"Even in tough times like these, Reed's endowment is on firm footing and it's largely because of John Gray."

John Gray reflected on his philanthropy in 2006, his 87th year.

"I made the money here (Pacific Northwest), I'll give most of it back, all of it probably. I feel strongly about that. I came from nothing, good parenting, good mother, we didn't have any money. My timing was good, I got a good education. I don't need it (the money). There are a lot of good causes I've been interested in. I have given away a lot, a great deal in fact. I will continue doing that."

The list of Gray's donations is long, millions every year, and much of it is done anonymously. Several foundations bear the Gray name.

CHAPTER 6

Developing the Spit

Salishan is a successful environmental project. Now it must be successful economically so that other people will use it as an example. We must prove that profit and beauty are compatible."

John Gray, 1963

The project (on Salishan Spit) gives one of the finest and worst examples of coastal development."

**Jim Ross, Deputy Director,
Land Conservation and Development
Commission (LCDC)**

The Arlington Club in Portland has a rich history. Formed in 1867 as 35 civic leaders in Portland put up $100 apiece to form the social club, the Arlington Club name derivation is unclear. Built in 1910 on Southwest Salmon Street, the men-only club catered to Portland's businessmen for decades until the men-only rule disappeared in later years. But in 1961 the club retained its male exclusivity and, on a winter day, the plans for Salishan were developed.

Saturday morning Dec. 30, 1961, and Salishan's four equal partners met at the Arlington Club in Portland along with Dave Pugh, architect manager of the Portland architectural firm of Skidmore, Owings and Merrill, and Bill Winters, representative of an advertising agency. The Salishan name came from Winters to identify the beach area, a reference to the language group of 97 Pacific Northwest tribes.

While it would be hard to imagine another name at this time, Gray had second-thoughts about the name as expressed in a March 1962 memo.

"It has been my experience that most people react unfavorably to it (the name) and that they must be sold on it," Gray said in the memo to his partners. "To most it is meaningless–they know nothing (of) Indian history and care less. I have to admit I'm swinging around to the idea we'd be better off using a truly descriptive name such as Sea Grove, Sea Forest, Sea Ridge or Ocean Grove."

But Gray's partners apparently liked the Salishan name and it stayed. It was later described in Oregon Geographic Names as "...an excellent example of a well-chosen name for a commercial development." (A name change survey of Salishan leaseholders in 1993 overwhelmingly favored keeping the name).

The well-known Salishan tree logo was later designed by Bill Erler, a Portland art director.

Gray had the vision for the property, ideas he roughed out in a July 1961 memo to his partners listing "Sea Ridge Development" as the subject.

Gray listed the following under the heading "General Features." Many of the concepts didn't make the cut but they underscored Gray's vision. (Parenthesis indicate author's comments)

1. Plan an area for a well-done resort type motel (Gray originally envisioned the "motel" on the west side of Highway 101).

2. Build a 9-hole full golf course with plans to add the second 9-holes later (completed)

3. Create a man-made lake adjacent to the highway (completed, later stocked with trout)

4. Provide tennis and badminton courts. (Outdoor tennis courts were built but not badminton)

5. Provide shuffleboard near the motel (didn't happen)

6. Lay out and provide several children's play areas, both in the commercial area and in the general housing area. (Some completed)

7. Construct at least one year-around covered swimming pool (completed)

8. Contract out the riding stable concession so that youngsters will have horses or ponies to ride. An existing barn (part of the Sijota buildings) may be ideal for this purpose.(not done–later planned for Immonen Road property but not completed)

9. Lay out various riding trails on the property (not done)

10. Lay out several hiking trails on the property and so mark them (some completed)

11. Provide an area for a general marina which might include Char-Broil type of restaurant for families (not done)

12. Design and construct an attractive stone and wood entrance marker and appropriate signs (not as recommended)

13. Possibly offer daily patrol service to absentee home owners (completed later)

14. Develop history of the immediate area as background data (unknown if completed)

15. Develop comparative average rainfall and temperature of this area as compared with Seaside and Gearhart (Oregon). Also, if available, get days of sunshine or fog on a comparative basis (unknown if completed).

Gray also gave a few guidelines for housing in the community.

1. Plan various areas so that we can satisfy various income levels and provide for them desirable sections (income levels were high)

2. Seriously consider a retirement colony or housing project in one area (not done)

3. Consider one area for co-op one story triplex-type homes with year-around maintenance, similar to many projects in Palm Desert and Palm Springs. (not done)

4. Utilize topsoil from the farm for the golf course and for house landscaping (unknown)

5. Have complete architectural control of all new home construction (completed)

6. Consider restricting use of any television antennas (done)

Adding to his memo, Gray also looked ahead to the future development of Salishan.

1. Activate interest in Taft as a small boat and fishing harbor and start work with the proper State and Government officials (not developed)

2. Consider the feasibility of a small general grocery and drug store near the present farm house or in our commercial area, wherever that might be (The Marketplace shopping center developed later)

3. Develop a definite motif for the entire project. Consider it along with the lines of a "Carmel" of the Northwest (referred to Carmel, California, the ultra-cute, ultra-chic oceanfront community used as a model of oceanfront development)

4. If possible, work out on house resale, so that our development corporation would have first refusal as resale agent on listing of homes (not done)

5. Consider the employment of a full-time handyman or carpentering, painting, plumbing, firewood, etc., and to bill services to the customers or at least be in the position to recommend reliable local specialists (not done)

6. Charge a flat yearly amount of $10 or $20 for community services for each house (completed)

7. Prohibit and or restrict removal or cutting of all trees and shrubs after the initial clearing (done)

8. Study the possibility of development of the property east of the highway as a home area and second golf course, together with another lake (future home of Salishan Lodge and second nine holes plus Salishan Hills)

The property was under the corporate ownership and the project began to move ahead quickly. In a 1972 interview, Gray described Salishan.

"It was the ideal piece of land which was not spoiled. We had a chance to get enough land along the highway to make some effort at controlling the environment and the approaches to the property, which you don't often get. And we had a chance to do what was way ahead of its time (1960); a planned unit development, protection of the bay and protection of the estuary, which no one thought about at that time."

The $10 million, 600-acre project was set to begin. Partners were assigned tasks at the December 1961 Arlington Club meeting. Paul Hebb would be on site with the land clearing details and sewage treatment plant development; Donald Drake would contact utilities, state highway commission; Russ Colwell, the financing arrangements; Gray the development of the corporate structure, development of a tax structure so the partners could get maximum capital gains benefits, and naming of the Salishan streets.

Salishan was ready to go.

Salishan Properties Inc. was incorporated as an Oregon corporation in January 1962. Of the 217 acres purchased from Hasselbrink, Frank Sijota, Dom DeBernardi and Emily Sijota, 112 acres were transferred to the corporation while the principals retained the balance. John Gray had already traveled throughout the United States looking at planned unit developments. The concept was new to Oregon and Gray was convinced he could do a better job than those he visited. In fact, Salishan would eventually become the first planned unit development in Oregon

William Wyse, involved with the development of Salishan, recalls Gray returning from those trips around the country to other developments and giving Wyse copies of all the brochures.

"John said 'I want something better than all of these.' That kind of puts you on the spot," Wyse said with a laugh during a 2004 interview.

Streets, public or private, became a key component in Salishan planning. Oregon law in 1962 stated that plats could not be approved unless streets were dedicated to public use without any restrictions. Salishan was a planned gated community and dedicating streets to the public didn't fit the gated community image.

William Wyse, a graduate of University of Washington and Harvard Law School, came to Portland in 1949. He had casual contact with John Gray in Portland for many years in Portland business circles but, in 1962, he was the real estate point man for the law firm later known as Stoel Rives and began working with Gray on Salishan and the unique lease arrangement.

"He (John Gray) would kind of get tired of things," Wyse recalled in 2003 interview. "He got tired of his chainsaw business.

He always had a yen to develop real property. He had a very, very good sense of what was good and what might actually go with people. He just loved this real estate thing"

Wyse called the lease arrangement "novel." But it didn't come without battling the Lincoln County attorney.

"The county took the view that no, if you have a subdivision, all the roads have to be public," Wyse recalled. The Salishan plan called for narrow streets and no sidewalks, a plan which the county would oppose had the streets been public.

But Wyse had a precedent in a small subdivision known as Wauna Lake east of Portland in Washington state near North Bonneville with approximately 50 cabins. Property was leased.

Wyse wanted to try the same thing at Salishan. All lease fees would be paid up front. Wyse's concept was that Salishan would be more a "shopping center" than a subdivision.

"You lease out buildings separately with a common area," Wyse said in describing the shopping center concept. "We floated the idea but the Lincoln County attorney said no and called the idea phony."

But the county attorney did agree that the idea could be submitted to the State of Oregon Attorney General Robert Thornton who happened to be an acquaintance of Wyse. The opinion came down in favor of Salishan and the leasehold concept was born.

"This arrangement (the streets) had me worried right up until the time we opened the site for leasing,"Gray said in 1962. "But Wyse assured us it was legal. We believe it is unique in Oregon":

For those contemplating building homes in the development, an architectural checklist in 1962 detailed restrictions. A sample from those restrictions:

Single story, required attached garages, exteriors indigenous to the Pacific Northwest; wood stains in lieu of paint. All building including remodeling, repainting, and fences submitted to architectural committee.

And while the Salishan spit construction was underway, plans were already being developed for the resort which would set Pacific Northwest standards for years to come. The local press reported plans for Salishan Lodge on July 19, 1964, with initial plans of 75 to 100 rooms. Announcement was made by Russell Colwell, president of Salishan Properties.

Site preparations on Salishan property began in January 1962 with some of the hill sites cleared. Architect Dave Pugh remembers trying to plow his way through 6-foot high salal and underbrush, taking a step, lying down to flatten the brush, taking another step and repeating the process.

"It took me half an hour to go 50-yards," he said.

Surveying lots was an adventure.

"We sort of did this thing by the seat of our pants," Pugh recalled. "We had an airplane survey by the Oregon Department of Transportation. That's the only map we had."

Pugh said he, architect Van Evera Bailey and the surveyors tried to follow the map in order to set lot lines. But the lot lines would be adjusted.

"If there was something like a beautiful tree that was on the line, we'd move the line, not the tree."

Pugh recalled a conversation with Van Evera Bailey as they took a coffee break. Bailey, who had a vacation home

From left to right, Russell Colwell, John Gray and Paul Hebb in this 1962 photo from Oregonian newspaper.

in Neskowin, a small village 15 miles north of Lincoln City, questioned the Salishan plan.

"Nobody will come down this far south," Bailey said as recalled by Pugh. "Neskowin is where everybody goes. Everybody who is anybody in Portland doesn't go south of Neskowin. This stuff (at Salishan) isn't going to be worth a damn."

Bailey would later buy a lot at Salishan.

The plan moved ahead.

"The idea (for Salishan) was to build it and have it look as much as it did before you got there as when you were finished.," Pugh said. "That was the general concept."

The initial plan also took into consideration location of the future hotel on the oceanfront and a proposed airstrip. Drawings included a road from Highway 101 along the bay and out the end of the spit where the hotel was planned. That plan would have required a revetment on the bay and filling. Later plans scrapped the airstrip, and the Lodge would be built on the east side of Highway 101.

Model homes drew buyers to Salishan Beach. Photo from Salishan promotional brochure.

The partners began their work.

"Paul Hebb became the point man on the site in early January 1962 and lived part-time in the old Sijota farmhouse," Gray recalled in a written recollection of the development. Betty Gray also brought her Girl Scout troops to the beach, the Sijota farmhouse serving as headquarters.

Hebb's assignments included bulldozing trails where roads would be constructed, clearing homesites and coordinating with various utilities. All utilities were to be underground. A dike along Siletz Bay was started in March and plans for the first nine holes of the golf course completed.

John Gray's budget for the Salishan project's first phase was $306,231 with $283,731 paid out in 1962 in initial development costs. These included clearing and readying of 140 to 150 lots, sewer and water connections to 50 percent of those lots, graveled roads, a sales office, golf shop, golf course maintenance building and the first 9-holes for the golf course. Golf course estimates were $140,315 for the course and related buildings.

Gray estimated a total return of $420,000 to $470,000 on land sales.

Early construction also used the talents of Barbara Fealy, a landscape architect from Portland who would make a major contribution to later construction of the Lodge.

In describing his plans for the property, Gray said "...it (the property) afforded our group an unusual opportunity to do the unusual."

Although the development would eventually become one of Oregon's higher priced developments, John Gray said it didn't start out that way.

"Our original efforts were for all kinds of housing. We had no minimum square footage," Gray said in 2005, noting that developers originally built smaller square footage homes. Gray admitted the development did end up with larger square footage houses, but was adamant that Salishan wasn't meant exclusively for the rich and famous.

Gray said he and his partners were originally concerned; would Salishan sell?

Owning land on both sides of Highway 101 was also a major factor as far as Gray was concerned "...so no hot dog stands, taverns or unwanted service stations can litter our immediate landscape." Gray pointed to other coastal areas such as Gearhart and Cannon Beach which were unzoned and "have grown in an unplanned manner."

The developers decided to have a separate sewage treatment facility as well as connecting with the local water district. Houses added later further north on the spit, not part of the original plan, would have septic systems. Depoe Bay Telephone Company was named as exclusive telephone provider.

By summer 1962 the sales efforts began with the first phase of 140 lots. But, at least in the opinion of William Wyse, the developers made a mistake by selling beachfront property first. By doing that and selling the inland lots later, the prime beachfront land went at less than market value.

Lot prices began in the $3,000 to $3,500 range with top oceanfront lots at $7,500. The cost included underground utilities, water, sewer and access to the Salishan Beach Club which, according to sales information, would offer swimming and tennis as soon as 25 homes were occupied or 125 lots sold. An annual upkeep charge not to exceed $100 was also included in lot sales. Financing was also offered with 25% down and balance within 3 years at 6% interest. Initially bank financing was a problem as banks were reluctant to loan funds on leased land. It took partner Russell Colwell's convincing argument to his employer, First

National Bank, to open the bank financing option and other banks soon followed.

Richard Livermore, plant engineer at Omark Industries, was named general manager for Salishan Properties. Livermore had handled property management for the Omark Profit Sharing Trusts.

The developers also wanted to make sure future homebuilders understood the Salishan restrictions. The concept of architectural controls was novel to the Coast and was defined by the developers in 1962 as follows;

"We desire to maintain, insofar as is possible, the natural character of this scenic land and to require that all man-made structures blend into the natural background rather than stand against it."

No views of trashcans or clotheslines at Salishan.

A winter storm in 1962 rearranged those trashcans.

In October 1962 a series of three storms blew into the Pacific Northwest. The first, relatively minor by comparison, hit the Oregon Coast on October 11, followed by the remnants of a tropical storm known as "Typhoon Freda" which dropped the barometer to a record 28.42. Columbus Day storm gusts at Mt. Hebo, northeast of Lincoln City, reached speeds of 131 mph before the anemometer disintegrated. The storm roared into the Willamette Valley with gusts in Portland reaching 116 mph. A third storm did little damage.

Touring Salishan the following weekend after the Columbus Day storm, John Gray found dozens of trees blown down and a sliding door in a model home blown out. A similar storm in 1981 cost Salishan leaseholders thousands in repair costs to Salishan Drive.

The first nine holes of the golf course would be completed by 1963. The developers committed to building a recreation building, designed by Dave Pugh, as well as a pool and tennis courts when the 25 homes were built or 125 lots sold, whichever came first.

Homesite prices ranged from $3,250 to $7,950. One year after initial construction had begun, 41 lots were sold, 50 lots by January 1963 including buyers from Portland (31), 5 other states and Canada. A second model home was under construction. By April 1963 the total number of lot sales stood 70. Actual home building was beginning on those lots with noted architects involved in what many considered to be the "architectural showplace of the Pacific Coast." A picnic in June 1963 further showed off the development and drew Oregon Gov. Mark Hatfield to the festivities (photo right: Hatfield seated  center, Mrs. Hatfield seated on left. Photo from Salishan leaseholders' newsletter).

Fiscal year sales summaries for Salishan by fiscal year showed Gray's optimism about Salishan was well- founded;

1962-1963 ; 41 homesites sold, average sales price of $5,244; 1963-1964; 28 homesites sold, average sales price of $6,128; 1964-1965; 36 homesites sold, average sales price of $6,491 1965-1966; 75 homesites sold, average sales price of $7,484.

While most of the buyers were from Oregon (41 out of the more than 50 originally sold), buyers from California, Washington, Colorado, Maryland and British Columbia also were among the original buyers.

J.W. "Wes" Lawyer was named general manager of Salishan Beach in 1964, replaced after short tenure by Orin Thresher in February 1965.

A DIFFERENT VIEW

There were those who didn't particularly share the Salishan vision. Robert Terrill, a retired foreign service officer who served on the leaseholders association for several years and had bought lots in 1962, wrote a lengthy recap of the first decade in Salishan history. It is interesting to view a different perspective.As recalled by Terrill, the Salishan roads were in constant state of disrepair with only one semi-paved road from 1962 to 1967. Others were rocked which resulted in winter mud and punctured tires while in the summer the "hordes of curiosity seekers" stirred up the dust.

"From its beginning in 1962 until mid-1967 Salishan had the atmosphere of a zoo," Terrill noted. Without restricted access the area youth found the beach access convenient for parties. The hiring of a "security officer" in 1964 by the developers, a man described by Terrill as "elderly" and "retreaded", wasn't successful, even after a car and a radio system ("on a 13-party circuit') were added. Terrill said the patrolman "remained invisible and incommunicado for all practical purposes."

Terrill noted the 1965 decision by the developers to abandon plans for the second nine of the golf course to extend northward and instead the sandspit opened for homesite development. Terrill said the decision would be fateful in later years as it was the starting point for Salishan Leaseholders Inc.

"If the golf course had been extended as originally intended, the roads of Salishan would as matter of commercial necessity been kept open to the public,' Terrill said. A result of this would be lack of privacy and "our properties could never have commanded premium prices."

Salishan wasn't built for low-income residents. Prominent names from Portland bought home sites including Phil Knight of Nike fame. The Robbins of Baskin-Robbins ice cream franchises found a home on the spit. John and Betty Gray's home commanded a Pacific view. Architect John Storrs designed and built his beachside retreat. He also designed two minimum square footage houses with the less than exciting name "Sali-Shantis."

Prominent Portland families such as the Naitos joined the Salishan land rush. A "beach cabin" at Salishan was the Portland status symbol for many years.

"Salishan has not violated nature," said state treasurer (and future Governor) Robert Straub said

The Longhouse condominiums, the first condos in Oregon. 1967 photo. Photographer unknown.

in 1970. "It is a perfect example of the goals planners must work toward in residential developments."

LEASEHOLDERS AND THE MARKETPLACE

In 1966 Salishan Drive and secondary roads were paved by developers and an entry gate installed. "Tranquility descended on the homeowners of Salishan,." Terrill said. Salishan was a hit. By July 1969 more than 300 home sites had been leased with 112 homes completed or under construction. The project was 75% complete. Salishan wasn't limited to single-family homes. The Longhouse, a seven-unit condominium, was unique in design as well as location. The term "Longhouse" is based on the Iroquian Indian name which implied "a large, elongated living structure which shelters several families." Built with 1964 dollars of $106,000 by Del Bennett of Newport and designed by the Portland architectural firm of Blair and Ziak, the apartment house had four, 2-bedroom, 2-bath, 1,887 square foot apartments and 3 one-bedroom apartments with 1,297 square feet. Sale prices ranged from $17,500 to $25,500 which included leasing a portion of the oceanfront property. Cedar shingles were used for the entire exterior as well as the roof. The uniquely designed building would later win prestigious awards from the Oregon chapter of the American, Institute of Architects (AIA) for architects Don Blair and Saul Zaik.

Another condominium development, the 11-unit Dune House, opened in 1967 with the first five units featuring ocean and mountain views. Designed by architects Bill Church and Roger Shiels, the units ranged in price from $23,950 to $28, 950 and were two or three-bedroom units

Development of the Marketplace, a small shopping mall on the west side of Highway 101, began in 1964, led by John Gray's guidance. Gray listed the following as "personal ideas" for the shopping center.

1. Center to be primarily convenience for residents of Salishan, Gleneden Beach and users of the Lodge.

2. No effort to attract a "Safeway operation.,'

3. Reasonable effort to attract tourists passing by but not through medium of standard signs such as "Dairy Queens" etc.

4. Keep the center small with open malls or paths and interesting landscaping.

5. Over period of time get people to stop because they heard it is attractive and unusual.

The Marketplace at Salishan, built at a cost of $1 million, wouldn't open until 1979.

In 1967 Barbara Fealy reviewed the Salishan development in a University of Oregon document.

"The soft light of the Oregon climate, the shadows of the forest, the driftwood colors of

1967 view of Salishan Spit.
Photo courtesy of Don Dagg.

the logs on the beach, contributed to the philosophy that all structures should unite with these elements into a harmonious oneness. All this adds up to the conviction that the preservation of natural beauty, the creation and maintenance of blending elements, is a major ingredient in successful developments. Salishan has changed the attitude of the Oregon coast. Salishan is indeed an environmental achievement."

While most of the statewide publicity surrounding Salishan was in a positive light during the 1960s, a series of winter storms and high surf in the early 1970s would suddenly threaten the development and send pricey homes into the sea.

CHAPTER 7

Slip-Sliding Away

"The Northwest Coast is one of the most dynamic environments in the world. Ocean waves and currents continuously reshape the shoreline. Portions of the beach are cut away while others are built out. Severe storms strike the coast during the winter, generating strong winds that drive rain against sea cliffs and homes and form huge ocean waves that crash against the shore. Beaches, giving way to waves and currents, retreat toward the land. At times this beach loss continues until the erosion threatens structures and cuts away at public parklands."

Coastal Natural Hazards
Oregon Sea Grant 1975

"New retirees arrive from the Midwest in summer to settle into the comfort of a beach home fronted by a wide beach, only to see the sand disappear next winter and the waves lapping at their doors."

Paul Komar

Will be like a foolish man who built his house upon the sand; and the rain fell, and the floods came, and the winds blew and beat against that house, and it fell and great was the fall of it."

Matthew 7:24-27

Michael Lockwood ended up in court for the right to build a second story on his oceanfront house at Salishan. Sued by three adjacent property owners who claimed their ocean views would be adversely affected, Lockwood would eventually be vindicated by the Oregon Supreme Court which ruled against the property owners. The court ruled the lease didn't prohibit a second story and even a one-story house would probably block the expensive views.

It didn't matter.

Within a few months the house, still under construction and valued in 1970 dollars at $60,000, would lie in a heap on the Salishan beach. Storm waves had eroded the sand beneath the house's concrete foundation. (Photo below, Statesman-Journal newspaper)

"Problems can usually be avoided if people will only recognize that the coastal zone is fundamentally different than inland areas and act accordingly," said Paul Komar in his book, "Pacific Northwest Coast; Living with the Shores of Oregon and Washington."

BAYOCEAN

When the sea remains relatively calm, currents predicable and winter storms mild, the danger is concealed. But, when a series of circumstances converge, the result can be devastating for oceanfront property owners. On the Oregon Coast the Bayocean development near Tillamook was a casebook example of what not to do on fragile spits surrounded by temperamental seas.

In 1906 Thomas Benton Potter, a successful real estate promoter and developer, saw the real estate sales potential of a four-mile long, 1,000-foot wide spit extending into Tillamook Bay with a point of land 140 feet above sea level. With a name of Bayocean and his son Thomas Irving Potter as the chief promotion man, the development had Atlantic City aspirations including a natatorium featuring "artificial surf" electronically generated. (For a complete account of Bayocean, the book by Bert Webber entitled "Bayocean: The Oregon Town that Fell Into the Sea" is the definitive description).

"Equating Salishan with Bayocean is most perceptive on Webber's part," said a state geologist in referring to Bert Webber's second book, "What Happened at Bayocean: Is Salishan Next?"

Schools, a hotel, road, a railroad and housing blossomed on the Tillamook Bay spit. Jetties were built, but between 1920 and 1925 the beach was disappearing. Once again a man-made jetty was creating a situation where erosion was cutting through the spit. The breach between the ocean and Tillamook Bay had occurred in 1948 after a severe winter storm and, as the Oregonian newspaper reported, "waves surged through this opening carrying salmon from the sea into the bay in six feet of water."

Eventually the beach erosion destroyed the town and buildings and Bayocean ended up as an island instead of a peninsula.

A Wakeup Call

The Siletz Spit had severe erosion problems but the causes were different from Bayocean. Instead of a jetty, a series of natural events combined to create a situation where ocean water could potentially enter Siletz Bay by cutting through the Salishan Spit.

"Oceanview." The term translates to premium prices, upscale residences and windows in constant need of washing. The demand for oceanfront lots on the Oregon Coast is high. Whether it's the lure of the Pacific or simply the one-upmanship of having an oceanfront vacation home, sales of oceanfront property were in full-swing by the early 1960s.

In less than 11 years after the bulldozers first cleared land on Salishan Spit, the ocean gave a wake-up call to those oceanfront landowners. Pristine beaches and dunes would be altered by huge boulders in efforts to stop the loss of land and newly-built homes.

The winter storms of 1972-1973 generated 23-foot waves combined with high tides, a combination which hit the Salishan Spit with full-force in December 1972. As the waves advanced eastward, the beach sand was washed away, clearing a path for a straight shot at the primary dune, a dune on which many of the houses were built.

A sand spit is a glorified sandbar, formed as sand is scooped up by the surf and deposited above a normal tide line. First comes the beach, followed by the primary dune, the secondary dune, the backdune and the bay.

"The primary dune is absolutely intolerant," according to Dr. Ian McHarg said in his 1971 book, "Design With Nature." "It (the primary dune) must be prohibited to use. If it is to be crossed.to reach the beach, it must be accomplished by bridges. As a consequence no development should be permitted on the primary dune, no walking should be allowed and it should not be breached at any point."

McHarg also recommended against using the secondary dune for any development, preferring the backdune as the preferred location for development.

"Sandbars are recent and ethereal," McHarg said. "There is no assurance that they will endure. There is no reason to believe the last storm was the worst."

An Oregon state geologist put it blunty.

"As a geologist, I wouldn't build a house there (Salishan)."

Those who did build houses hit by the December 1972 events braced themselves as the 8.9 to 9.1-foot tides of February 1973 were anticipated and houses perched precariously on the sand dune.

Any storm activity combined with those February tides could breach Salishan Spit and pour ocean water into Siletz Bay, an occurrence not considered ecologically unsound in the opinion of some fish and game officials who said the intrusion of the ocean might clear out the silt and revitalize the bay's salinity. But opinions were mixed in that debate

State and local officials prepared for the worst.

A representative of the Army Corps of Engineers took a pessimistic view.

"If what Oregon coastal experts predict—that a high tide will breach the spit on or about Feb. 15--- is true, I don't see any possibility of doing anything about it, at least from our standpoint," said Corps spokesman Lt. Col. Paul Driscoll.

Efforts to save beachfront property took on new urgency and Gov. Tom McCall ordered emergency action. Concern ranged from saving the Salishan homes to the effect a breach would have on Cutler City, a low-lying part of the mainland on the northeastern shores of Siletz Bay.

The Salishan Spit was in danger of being breached in three areas, two on the ocean side and one on the bay side.

McCall appointed a team led by Oregon State University dean of engineering Fred Burgess to study immediate remedies to the problem and to find a long-term solution to further erosion. McCall promised to seek emergency federal aid through Sen. Mark O. Hatfield.

It appeared rip-rapping would be the choice for oceanfront property owners. Rip-rapping involves dumping enormous boulders in front of the dunes, dissipating the power of the onrushing waves. John Gray was the first homeowner to protect his land with rip-rap. But behind the scenes a political move by some homeowners angered just about everyone in Salishan without oceanfront land.

The group asked legislators to introduce a bill in the state legislature which would allow a "Public Diking District," a local taxing district under the jurisdiction of the Lincoln County Board of Commissioners which would have the power to levy taxes on all Salishan properties as a way to finance protective structures on the beach.

Cost of those protections ranged upwards to $10 million plus annual maintenance costs of $1 million. According to leaseholder Robert Terrill, the huge rocks needed for the rip-rapping would have to be trucked across Salishan roads and the roads would eventually open to the public.

Suddenly, however, the diking plan went public and was subsequently opposed by Salishan property owners, especially those on higher ground without danger from the erosion. The ensuing controversy nearly generated impeachment proceedings against Salishan board members. One board member resigned.

The state legislature was split on whether to consider any funding for the spit.

"I wonder if there no expensive homes on the sandspit whether there would be talk of spending state dollars to keep the sand in place," said Sen. Bill Stevenson (D-Portland) in 1973.

The diking district proposal died in the legislature as legislators noted that diking districts were limited to privately owned properties. Technically, Salishan property was leased. But, at least in Terrill's opinion, the episode "...ended once and for all attempts to split the leaseholders into two antagonistic groups consisting of those inhabiting the sandspit and those secure in the uplands."

In a flurry of activity during February in anticipation of the high tides, more rip-rap was dumped on the Salishan beaches. In Salem, Gov. McCall announced no dollars were available from state or federal sources to protect the private property. Earlier discussion of assistance brought angry responses from many Oregonians who saw Salishan as a rich, gated enclave which shouldn't be rescued with tax dollars.

Why was the winter of 1972-1973 so severe in terms of erosion? Paul Komar and C. Cary Rea,, in their study entitled "The Causes of Erosion of Siletz Spit', pinpointed a couple a major causes. Foremost, rip currents established offshore can clear the way.

"The rip current hollowed out a large embayment on the beach, entirely removing the portion of the beach above high tide level so that wave swash was able to reach the dunes," according the report. "The loose sands, offering no resistance to the waves, were easily eroded away.'

Erosion was localized. One property was spared while adjacent land was reclaimed by the sea.

Komar and Rea noted another circumstance which, in their opinion, may have had a significant impact on the erosion; sand mining operations by Oceanlake Sand and Gravel on a beach at School House Creek one and one-half miles south of the spit. According to the report, more than 111,000 cubic yards of sand were removed between 1965 and 1971. Coincidentally, Oceanlake was owned by Lyle Hasselbrink, the owner of much of the property sold earlier to the John Gray partnership for the Salishan development.

"...removal of the sand by mining operations probably disrupted the natural balance of beach sand, the balance of sand gains and losses on the beach," the report noted. "With a decreased volume the beach was not able to protect the coastal property from wave attack, and accelerated erosion resulted."

"The mining operations aggravated the situation and caused increased erosion."

The mining was later stopped.

The Salishan spit has limited sources of replenishment, chiefly coarse sand derived from erosion of sea cliffs. According to the report, the Siletz River carries finer sands which remain in the estuary and do not replenish the beach. Columbia River sand is blocked by the rocky headlands. In other words, sources of sand for the Siletz Spit were few and far between, most of it coming from erosion of sea cliffs.

A waterfront study group, part of the leaseholders association, also pointed to another possible cause for the erosion, especially the erosion on the bay side of the spit. Millport Slough, a 75-foot wide branch of the Siletz River, provided an escapement for regularly occurring Siletz River floods and also created a counter-current for the westerly flow of the river. But several years earlier Lincoln County removed a bridge and filled in a portion of the slough to provide county road access from Immonen Road to property behind where the Lodge is currently located. The dike was removed in 1981 and replaced with a bridge.

"Recent landfills in Siletz Bay have probably aggravated the erosion problem," according to the Komar report. "Prior to these fills, flood waters would flow in part into the south bay and dissipate the energy of the flood waters. Now that this spill is prevented by fills, the full flood discharge of the Siletz river is directed toward the back of the spit, into the area that is eroding."

Developments such as Siletz Keys and probably Salishan Spit would be prohibited today with Oregon's tight land-use laws although those laws have been constant attack in the recent years.

The study group also strongly opposed any jetty construction, a proposal floated by the U.S. Corps of Engineers.

"According to highly qualified sources," the board noted, "the result (of the jetty) could be fatal to our beachfront."

The Corps eventually abandoned the idea of jetties.

Saving the Salishan beachfront prompted some unusual proposals. Building a permanent revetment along the beach (at a cost of $800,000 per mile) or pumping sand from the ocean floor to the beach through 6-inch pipes were schemes by the US Corps of Engineers. Both of those solutions were also scrapped.

February 1973. While more property without rip-rap protection was lost to the sea, the spit survived as moderate seas prevailed. But the acres of rip-rap had permanently altered the beach architecture and given Salishan Spit a different appearance. As sand and driftwood backfilled behind the rip-rap, the rocks disappeared and looking at the spit on most days today gives no indication of any prior problems. But with the Oregon Coast retreating as much as 2 feet per year and that retreat sometimes accelerated by rip-rap, future problems may lie ahead. In less than 3 weeks in 1972, for example, 100-feet of of Siletz Spit disappeared.

But even the erosion had a positive economic impact for Salishan homeowners as the Lincoln County Assessor's office gave a 25% reduction in assessed valuation due to "erosion damage." The reduction applied to properties north of the narrowest portion of the spit.

While not mentioned in the Salishan homesite sales literature for obvious reasons, another major threat to Salishan and the Oregon Coast is the tsunami or the misnamed tidal wave. A major earthquake estimated at 9-plus magnitude hit off the Oregon Coast on January 26, 1700 and generated 50-foot waves into Siletz Bay and along the coastline, destroying Indian homesites and killing dozens.

Generated by earthquake activity on the ocean floor, part of the Cascade Subduction Zone, the seismic waves can travel up to 600 miles per hour, slamming into the coastline with waves as high as 100 feet. A 1964 seismic event in Alaska sent waves onto a beach 15 miles south of Salishan, sweeping four children into the sea where they drowned.

A major tsunami today would wipe Salishan Spit clean.

Tsunamis, erosion and hurricane force winds during the winter storms; the forces of nature meet Salishan head-on. Thus far Salishan has survived mostly intact. But many geologists, climatologists and oceanographers are watching the Salishan Spit carefully.

The erosion issue went to court in 1973 as a class action lawsuit was filed against Salishan Properties Inc., John Gray and Russell Colwell. The suit, filed in Multnomah County Circuit Court, contended the defendants knew or should have known the Salishan lots would be damaged or destroyed by erosion and other water adjacent to the lots.

The suit went on to say that the defendants falsely represented to them that lots were situated on an "ancient sand dune" that had been building for centuries.

A Multnomah County judge ruled the class action improper and the plaintiffs immediately filed individual complaints although the ruling was appealed.

One of the cases reached a jury trial in 1976 and the Multnomah County jury ruled in favor of Salishan Properties in the case although 39 other suits were still pending (the Oregon

Supreme Court upheld a previous ruling that separate actions should be considered instead of a class action). The jury had ruled on a case of Wade V. Cook who was seeking damages of $30,237, noting that the warranty did not extend to an unimproved seashore lot that eventually eroded.

An appellate court ruled in favor of Salishan in August 1985 and the Oregon Supreme Court denied review of the case in December 1985.

The remaining cases were dropped.

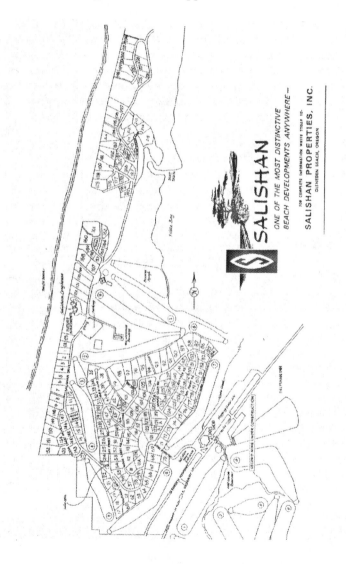

CHAPTER 8

Years on the Spit

"The land here is of a type of scenic beauty that had to get the best development treatment,"

John D. Gray

Dreams of a home by the sea came true for Salishan leaseholders as the development caught the imagination of many upscale buyers during the 1960s and 1970s and the bare lots became homesites. For one leaseholder, however, a lifelong dream ended up smashed to bits on the Salishan beach.

Marshall James, a Salishan homeowner, wanted to sail around the world. With a special permit granted by Salishan Properties in 1963 James was granted permission for a temporary boat shed where he planned to build his 45-foot ketch. The permit noted that the boat shed "will be sited so as to minimize its visibility."

James' dream of sailing away into the sunset was close. The former Salishan Properties manager had sold his Salishan house, and his 47-foot ferro-cement schooner was ready to move. In October 1972 the boat moved slowly up Salishan Drive on a flatbed trailer, through the Salishan entry gate after the center post of the gate mechanism was removed, and then north on Highway 101 to Siletz Keys where a crane would lift the vessel into Siletz Bay.

The "Marjean" was outfitted with masts at Siletz Keys and readied for an extended world voyage: the Galapagos Islands, the warm South Seas and beyond.

On December 31, 1972, the "Marjean" left the Siletz Bay estuary under engine power, crossed the bar and pointed west. Two years of work ended in 40-minutes as sand jammed the exhaust system and the engine failed. The sailboat was pushed into the Salishan beach where the hull cracked.

Bulldozers would later break up the boat after the masts and other equipment had been removed. Remains of Marshall James' dream were buried in the Salishan beach sand. A $100,000 insurance settlement was questioned because James had reportedly failed to secure a proper Coast Guard inspection.

GOLF

"The land here is of a type of scenic beauty that had to get the best development treatment," Gray said in 1962, referring to the golf course project. The following golf definition captured the Salishan plan:

links - 1. originally referred to seaside courses, now used loosely to mean any golf course. 2. ("links style course", "links course") an exposed, windswept (sometimes seaside) course characterized by gently rolling mounds/dunes and very few (if any) trees. Often the ninth hole is not near the clubhouse but in fact one of the farthest points from the clubhouse on the course.

Although room revenues were the top revenue producing line item in future Salishan Lodge budgets, the golf course was second and generated many of those extra room nights, "heads on beds" in the sales department slang. The promise of golf also accelerated lot sales on the spit. As with the rest of the Salishan development the golf course would not be the standard model.

Oregon resident Fred Federspiel, golf course architect and construction supervisor, was well-known in the Pacific Northwest. Federspiel's credits included Royal Oaks in Vancouver, Wa; Meriwether, Springfield Country Club, Lake Oswego County Club and a newly constructed course in Florence, Or.

The first nine holes of the golf course would be completed by 1963. The course was in "links" style, a close relative of the Scottish courses highlighted by gently rolling mounds and dunes, windswept and with roughs. The following was a description of the Salishan Golf Links as described in a golf magazine;

"This course (Salishan) is a reflection of the Scottish tradition. In Scotland, some golf links are built upon land reclaimed from the sea. The Pacific Ocean and Siletz Bay line the majority of the northwest corner of this course. Water hazards come into play on five holes. The rugged and natural beauty of the

78

terrain combined with all the weather elements will provide even the best golfer with a challenging round.

Locals say that this course has been created in harmony with nature. The trees and coastal vegetation surrounding the areas of play are left as natural as possible. As on Scottish-links courses, the tee boxes, landing areas and greens are well-maintained. The forest and brush on the sides of the fairways will make finding an errant ball almost impossible. Hitting straight shots is important when playing this course. Many of the greens are mounded, making shot placement all the more vital. Due to the pine tree formations, there are many dogleg fairways that require players to use caution or find themselves looking at possible double bogies. The well-bunkered greens also add to the difficulty.

EAST VS. WEST

By August 1963 the developers were debating where the second nine holes should go, some arguing for going north to Siletz Bay while others favored the east side of Highway 101 and using the Sijota tunnel under the highway.

Gray listed the pros and cons of both sides of the highway. Among the pros for taking the next 9 holes north on the spit included a "Pebble Beach flavor" and enhancing homesite values on the spit. But the cons were mainly expense including a "diking job" on Siletz Bay, high cost of topsoil and "too many golf balls in yards". Among the positive arguments for the east side were less fog, more visibility from Highway 101, keeping "transient" traffic out of the residential area and more room for wider fairways.

The east side won, making the existing nine holes the back nine, converting the first pro shop into the community building, building a new driving range on the east side and building a new pro shop at the present location on Highway 101.

Built prior to the Tiger Woods-generated golf boom of the late 1990s, the Salishan golf course was immediately hailed as "The Pebble Beach of the Pacific Northwest." The first nine holes on the east side of Highway 101, opened for play in summer 1963, and were inaugurated by a pro-am invitational tournament which featured 20 pros and 60 amateurs led by Portland television station KGW-TV's sportscaster Doug LaMear with a 76 for low amateur honors. The par-72, 3,121-yard course challenged the golfers.

Pete Cline, the course's first golf professional, said in 1963 "the Salishan course is very interesting because no two holes are alike. It's very scenic and there's a little breeze blowing at all times to keep the average golfer on his toes. The facilities are extremely well-planned. The pro shop will have complete accommodations for display and work areas and we intend to carry a complete stock of top quality golf equipment and accessories."

Cline, 32 years old, had been the assistant professional at the upscale Waverly Country Club in Portland for nine years prior to his Salishan assignment, his first head professional job. (photo right–from Salishan newsletter)

In late 1963 bulldozers were clearing land on the east side of Highway 101 in preparation for the second nine holes of the Salishan golf course, a par 36, 3,217- yard course. Lot sales were brisk on the west side as 80 lots were leased by the end of the year. Salishan even offered a financing plan: ESWYPP, "Enjoy Salishan While You Pay Plan." Most of the buyers weren't in need of financial assistance.

By 1964 John Gray was anxious to see the golf pro shop relocated. There was even consideration of lighting the driving range at night but the idea was never realized. The new pro shop would be built on the west side of Highway 101 with easy accessibility from the busy highway. A coffee shop would be included in the design. The old pro shop would be turned into a community recreation center with a 25x50 swimming pool in the plans.

The $100,000, 4,275 square foot pro shop, designed by Dave Pugh and his associates at Skidmore, Owings and Merrill, and in keeping with the concepts of Salishan, would feature an interior of cedar paneling and exposed wood deck, ceilings and beams. (drawing top of next page)

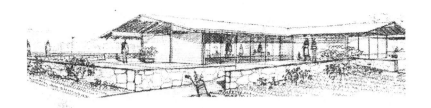

The golf course was leased in 1972 to Lee-Lyons Inc. of Portland and Clark Cumpston and Ron Manougian were named teaching professionals. Pete Cline resigned. The lease was short-lived. Grant Rogers served as golf professional for several years before joining former Salishan general manager Hank Hickox at Bandon Dunes.

The tennis courts were ready for play, surrounded by 12-foot high cedar posts and wire fencing.

Substantial fire insurance premiums were a surprise to some Salishan owners, a situation alleviated by the later construction of a fire station in Gleneden Beach

An additional 30 homesites were opened for sale on the Spit. A survey of current leaseholders in 1964 showed nine doctors, seven attorneys, three realtors, three architects, a pharmacist, contractor and engineer were among the leaseholders. A second model home was sold. Plans for new homes were swamping the architecture review committee.

By 1965 the big news was across Highway 101 as Salishan Lodge neared the grand opening in July.

Of the original 219 homesites more than two-thirds had been leased. The Longhouse won a prestigious award from the Oregon chapter of the American Institute of Architects. Completion of the community club, formerly the golf pro shop, was completed as was the swimming pool while the new pro shop was nearing completion.

LEASEHOLDERS

In 1966 the Salishan leaseholders decided a permanent organization of the Leaseholders was in the future and organized a "founding committee" to begin negotiations with Salishan Properties Inc. New directors of the Salishan Leaseholders were: Edward Cooley, Lyle Hasselbrink, Elwood Hedberg, Peter Inglis, Robert Martin, Raymond McGrew and Robert Terrill. Terrill, a retired foreign service officer, was named chairman. Salishan Leaseholders acquired Oregon corporate status in October 1966.

An electronic entry gate became the big news for the Leaseholders in 1967 along with a new cable TV system as the group celebrated its one-year anniversary. With total income of $26,950 from fees and interest, estimated expenditures were approximately $19,931 with community club expenses, especially the swimming pool, topping the expenditure ledger followed by maintenance of Salishan Drive, the main roadway in the development.

An update in 1968 provided the following information on homesite sales:

Number of homesite platted: 315
Number of homesites leased: 282
Designated condominium sites: 4
Estimated maximum number of future homesites: 120 to 130

An experimental "boat basin" was cut into the spit with future plans of access into the Siletz River. Preliminary studies began for a shopping center.

The surrounding area was also undergoing changes in 1968. An airport was under construction south of Salishan Lodge. A Highway 101 bypass proposal in Lincoln City began the hearing process, a bypass which never happened as traffic to this day crawls through the middle of the town. A new hospital, North Lincoln, opened in Lincoln City with two Salishan leaseholders as active members of the hospital board; Robert Terrill and Jack Brady.

The Leaseholders decided in 1969 to hire a manager and fellow leaseholder Marshall James was named to the post with an annual salary of $6,300. Transfer of Salishan to the Leaseholders also neared completion as Leaseholder and board member(soon to be elected chairman) Howard Rankin, a Portland attorney, oversaw the transfer.

Security was always an issue at Salishan and, in 1969, the Board decided to hire its own security individual rather than use the services of a Portland company. While the security man would routinely patrol Salishan, individual Leaseholders could pay an additional $25 for "frequent periodic exterior inspection" of a residence.

Homesite sales continued in 1970 with oceanfront lots ranging from $18,000 to $22,500. Bay view lots ranged from

$4,950 to 11,500. Some completed homes went on the market; a three-bedroom, two bath fully furnished ocean view houses was marketed at $59,500, while a 3-bedroom, 2 batch home with 4 fireplaces was sold at $65,000. Some recent Salishan sales in 2005 are nearing the $1 million mark.

Robert Terrill, a leaseholder but not a fan of Salishan Properties, recalls the initial formation of the Leasholders organization in his publication "Salishan Leaseholders Inc: The First Decade." Gray laughingly recalled Terrill as "a pain in the neck for everybody" but said Terrill was also a family friend who taught Gray's son how to fly fish and tie flies.

"Two years of hassling with the evasive owners of Properties then ensued in an endeavor by Salishan Leaseholders to assume all managerial functions and ownership of Salishan's leased homesites," Terrill said. "On August 20, 1969, an agreement of limited scope was finally concluded whereby S.L.I. on January 1, 1970, would legally assume all duties and responsibilities relating to the maintenance fund monies and custody thereof."

On January 1, 1970, Salishan Leaseholders Inc. took over management duties of the spit land from Salishan Properties Inc. although the Properties maintained the architectural committee. Leaseholders were an active organization with committees ranging from environmental protection to recreation to grounds and security. The brief stint of manager Bob Aplet was ended in 1971 and Jean Streun was named acting manager and controller. Streun resigned in 1972, replaced by current manager Tom Trunt. Facing increased maintenance costs the Board raised the fee to $199.50 in 1971. Gregory Killpack was named recreation director.

Salishan residents were a politically active group, whether responding to a proposed Siletz River bridge in 1971 or additional dredging in the bay. A proposal by Oregon Department of Transportation in 1970 would have allowed motor vehicles on the Gleneden Beach and nearby beaches. The Salishan residents, by a vote of 160 to 6, made it clear this wasn't acceptable.

"Salishan is synonymous with the best in land development and is a source of pride to the state," noted the Salishan newsletter. "It is ironic that an area so carefully planned and dedicated to the preservation of the natural environment should be singled out for an activity so alien to nature."

The highway department backed off.

In 1970 Hollywood came to Salishan as the filming of Ken Kesey's "Sometimes a Great Notion" sent locals into celebrity worship mode as Paul Newman and his wife, Joanne Woodward, and their seven children rented a home on Salishan as did Henry Fonda and his wife, Shirlee. Fonda and Lee Remick roamed through the various Lincoln County filming locations, and Marlon Brando made a visit to the Newman's at their Salishan rental. From South Beach near Newport to Toledo to a false front house on the Siletz River representing the fictional Stamper home, the appearance of Hollywood stars sent residents into a front-page tizzy as reported by the Newport News-Times. Weeks of front-page coverage included interviews, house decorating tips from the movie's set designer and numerous photos.

"Sometimes a Great Notion" was released in 1971 and was the first movie HBO aired when the pay service premiered in 1972. A television series, "Knots Landing" would use Salishan Lodge for location in later years.

Building on the spit came to halt in 1972 as it did throughout Lincoln County as Gov. Tom McCall, disgusted with Lincoln County's well-documented planning deficiencies and the raw sewage spilling onto the beaches, stopped all building in the county. McCall described the issues in his autobiography.

"The most abused land in Oregon is on the central coast. Developers carved it up with a buffalo hunter mentality. Lincoln City was a model of strip city grotesque. By the fall of 1972, the pelt skinners had moved in for the kill. Local officials had approved a subdivision of 1,400 lots with a drain field area for only 600 houses. Thirty-nine of the 60 water systems did not meet state standards. Department of Environmental Quality inspectors found 34 cases of raw sewage flowing onto the beach. I declared a moratorium of construction in Lincoln County, which brought heated protest from developers and real estate salesmen. But it sent a message that hucksterism in land sales would not be tolerated."

By September 1975 the Salishan Leaseholders were ready to request transference all rights and title in Salishan's residential area from Salishan Properties to Salishan Leaseholders. The final agreement provided S.L.I. with office space and land near the entry gate and agreement to hold the Leaseholders harmless in the event of future lawsuits regarding "structural defect" in the residential land (erosion). The agreement was approved.

The houses of Salishan line the east bank of Siletz Bay.

"In summary," Robert Terrill said, "within less than 10 years of its founding, S.L.I. had become master in its own house and embarked on a unique experiment in representative self-government by the leaseholders, vested with broad powers of control over a corporation owning the lands underlying their estates, together with all amenities and appurtenances."

All was not smooth statewide as the Land Conservation and Development Commission (LCDC) began flexing its bureaucratic muscles. A "guideline" (Goal 18) in land use planning restricted further building on the Spit in 1977, a ruling appealed to the Lincoln County Commissioners. Salishan owners would file suit against Lincoln County in 1978. Lincoln County Circuit Court Judge A.R. McMullen ruled for Salishan in June 1978. The judgment was followed by a Lincoln County Commissioner dictate that building could continue on the spit if land was properly rip-rapped.

John Gray had other developments in the works during the first years of Salishan. Sunriver, another well-recognized name in Oregon., was originally 5,500 acres owned by the U.S. Government and housed Camp Abbot, a training camp for the U.S. Army. The Great Hall at Sunriver served as the officer's club. Gray and his partner, Don McCallum, bought the property in 1965, named it Sunriver, sold the first homesite in 1968, and developed the land into what today is recognized as a top destination resort in the Pacific Northwest.

Gray would form another partnership in Portland in 1971, Macadam Investors, and develop 35-acres on the banks of the Willamette River known as Johns Landing. Land acquisition for the project had begun in 1968.

Prior to all of his later developments the one which stood out in Oregon history was across Highway 101 from the Salishan Spit—Salishan Lodge.

CHAPTER 9

Taking Form

"Complete privacy. View of the bay. It is like stumbling into your dreams. A place you know exists but you can't find."

John Storrs, 1965

"Salishan is meant to bring one closer to nature where we can witness the gigantic forces of the sea and the forest and the great beauty of Oregon. It is hoped that all who come here will be renewed by the experience of being in the midst of giant sruces, hemlocks, firs and pines, by the sound and smell of the surf, by the sight of the cranes in the marshes and of the sandpipers on the beach. "

Barbara Fealy, 1964

Where rainbows bend across the heavens, where guests arrive as young lovers and later return as grandparents.

Jerry Hulse, Los Angeles Times, 1991

By the summer of 1961, within months of finalizing the various property purchases including the spit, preliminary plans were already underway for a"resort-type motel" with initial siting on the west side of Highway 101. But John Gray, after purchasing property on the east side, decided the Lodge would be better suited on that side of the highway for a variety of reasons including keeping the golf course and Lodge traffic away from the residential area. Critics said the decision was the wrong one; building a resort on the Coast had to be on the ocean. Ocean view was different than oceanfront. The success of Salishan Lodge would prove the critics wrong.

Gray immediately selected Portland architect John Storrs to lead the design teams.

"Salishan is an architect's dream", Storrs said in 1965, the year the Lodge opened. "It's not often a man will say to you, 'Here's $2 million. Give me a building."

The building, rising from Storrs' imagination, was unlike any other on the Coast.

"It was our intention to build a heavy timber and sloping roof building (for the central lodge) that looked as though it belonged on the Oregon Coast," Storrs said. "The main lodge is kind of monumental, but not something that scares people away and completely constructed of wood and local products. The furnishings are good, but not overpowering. The paintings and art work will be local, and capture the feeling of the area."

In another interview in 1965, Storrs said "we want this Lodge to appear as though it had been dropped into the woods."

It was John Gray's vision which led Storrs in many directions. A 1964 memo to Storrs, partner Russell Colwell and Salishan Properties manager Dick Livermore detailed Gray's vision of Salishan Lodge (author's notes in parenthesis).

1. Probably 40-50 units at start with provision for substantial expansion (eventually 210 rooms)

2. Entrance will be in past driving range parking area (this was when the Lodge was originally proposed for the west side of Highway 101)

3. Sign on or visible from highway for vacancy or "Sorry" sign switched from manager's office (not used)

4. Distinctive entrance area such as open pitched beams or poles to indicate registration (designed by Storrs)

5. Manager's apartment (not used)

6. Pool area. Glass in and make provision so can be covered (completed)

7. A sauna room (completed)

8. Consider an area for apartment rentals to local people such as teachers (not completed although a later apartment building was built for Salishan employees)

9. Master plan to include provision for a restaurant if airport does not develop or if demand overwhelms us (two restaurants, The Sun room and The Gourmet Room included)

10. Design concept to be truly Northwest–don't try to be Tahiti, etc. Put our best foot forward.

11. This particular motel shouldn't be overly plush. Save that for the oceanfront if it develops. This should be economical to build and maintain so rates can be competitive. Still must be distinctive and offer the vacationers and golfers a real reason for coming back.

12. Study 2-story view buildings vs. 1-story arrangement of Vacation Village. 2-story perhaps better for views unless can group carports out of sight line.

13. May necessitate a sewage treatment plant on east side (later built)

14. Features of rooms: decks or patios, fireplaces in all (done) b. covered carports grouped with covered walks (done) c. kitchenettes in all, perhaps in between some units so flexible (not done)

15. Conference area or room which could double for activity, art classes, movies, etc. At start could be part of motel with idea of partitioning into motel units and building a separate conference center (meeting and conference space built) ; b. toilets and perhaps a kitchen area so could cater to women's clubs, etc. (not done); c. blackboards and screens (incorporated into conference center)

16. Probably phones and switchboard (done)

17. TV cable in (done)

18. Imaginative landscaping and site plan (Barbara Fealy responsibility)

19. Really study heat problem so as to get low cost. Consider oil and hot water, maybe off pool heater. (Not done–a handwritten comment to the side of this suggestion; "HA!)

Storrs had his blueprint and named his general contractor, Del Bennett of Newport. Next, and probably most importantly, came the selection of Barbara Fealy as the landscape architect.

"The grading concept was to blend the area back into the forest," Fealy said. "This allowed for much undulation in form. Berms and hummocks were created as barriers and blinds and offer privacy between guest units, and to shield the playground and parking lots. Plant material consisted of native plants, especially the broad leafed evergreens and confiers with which Oregon is greatly endowed. Gaultheria shallon (salal), Vaccinimum ovatum (huckleberry) Myrica californica (wax myrtle), Pinus contorta (Coast pine) Tsuga heterphyylla (western hemlock), Mahonia aquifolium (Oregon grape), Acer circiniatum (vine maple) were typical of the richness and variety used.

All this adds up to the conviction that the preservation of natural beauty, the creation and maintenance of blending elements, is a major ingredient in successful developments. Salishan has changed the attitude of the Oregon coast. Salishan is indeed an environmental achievement."

The Oregon Association of Nurserymen's Award of Merit, the first of its kind in Oregon, went to Salishan Lodge shortly after the Lodge opened in 1965. The award cited Salishan for "its outstanding contribution to the beautification of the State of Oregon, and in recognition for its preservation of plant life in its natural habitat for the benefit of all."

CONSTRUCTION BEGINS

With Barbara Fealy at the landscaping helm and Storrs guiding the main building construction with builder Del Bennett, the Lodge began construction in October 1964. Thirteen of the original guestrooms were fabricated at an off-site location. More than 125 construction workers were employed.

Storrs had ordered the following; 490,300 board feet of Douglas Fir framing, 286,420 board feet of Douglas Fir timbers, 348,000 board feet of 3x6 Hemlock decking, 53,000 board feet of 2x6 Hemlock decking, 28,600 board feet of finish lumber, 53,000 board feet of exterior cedar siding and paneling, 180,000 square feet of Douglas Fir construction grade plywood, and 123,000 square feet of Douglas Fir specialty plywood.

"Virtually every room in the lodge contains some wood products either in a decorative or structural manner", according to a wood products magazine from 1965.

Storrs' propensity for natural woods would show everywhere in the Lodge; walnut and oak throughout the lobby, eight-sided Hemlock columns in the coffee shop, 13 teakwood panels designed by Portland artist LeRoy Setziol, Western Red Cedar shingles in the Attic Lounge, teak handrails, teak paneling and Portuguese cork in the board room.

"It is certainly one of the most beautiful modern hotels I have ever seen anywhere in the world," according to San Francisco Examiner writer Kenneth Roxroth. ""Yet the architecture is not only extremely Oregonian, in a style of modern wooden construction and organization of profiles and masses; (Salishan Lodge) may well become a special contribution of the state to the history of architecture."

Salishan Lodge "...will be a facility of which Oregon can be proud," John Gray said in January 1965, shortly after construction began. "It will reflect the spectacular beauty of its coastal setting and in itself will be an attraction which will bring visitors to the state and enhance Oregon's important tourism industry."

The planned 96 guest rooms were spacious in comparison to other "motels"--16 by 26 feet-- and featuring complete soundproofing, Acrilan wall to wall carpeting, wood paneling, masonry fireplaces with raised hearths, tile bathroom floors and custom designed bed headboards. The rooms in 12 separate buildings were built in cluster units of eight with four rooms upstairs and four downstairs, all connected to the central Lodge with shake-covered walkways as well as a connected carport. 60 of the rooms would have two, extra-length double beds, 24 rooms with king-sized beds and 12 studio rooms had sofabeds. A thirteenth building would house 4, two-bedroom units.

"The decision was made at the very beginning to have individual, covered, numbered parking for every room, and we knew there'd be a lot of motors warming up, so soundproofing was vital," manager Alex Murphy said in 1981. "John Gray asked me to write down a list of items that rooms should have, in order of importance. I wrote down number one, soundproofing; number 2, soundproofing; number three, soundproofing."

Connecting the buildings on the rainy Oregon Coast would be covered walkways built with 2x12 rough-cedar construction.

"Although we didn't build them (the covered walkways) instantly, as soon as we got open we knew we must have covered walkways," Murphy said in 1981. "At first they were drawn with cedar shakes on them, like the rest of the buildings. But someone brought up the idea of making them a little different, and we went to this 2x12 rough cedar construction. It would cost a million dollars to build them today. It's noticed too, especially people who know construction and architecture. They say incredulously, "Is that really 2x12 cedar?"'

Overnight guests were the target audience but Lodge developers also recognized the growing conference business and included a separate building connected to the Lodge with facilities for serving 200 attendees at banquets with conversion to three smaller rooms. The building was called the Council House. In the era prior to electronic devices, Salishan was proud to advertise that the conference center had easels, blackboards as well as controlled lighting and sound systems. Guest rooms would have a television and a telephone. Additional meeting space, the Lincoln and Pine rooms, could accommodate up to 60 persons.

Within the main Lodge, a double stone fireplace would welcome guests as they walked across a Montana mica stone floor to the registration desk constructed of walnut and oak. Upstairs, The Attic Lounge, featuring an entire wall covered with Western red cedar shingles, would offer entertainment and The Gallery Room would display art shows, informal entertainment and movies. Describing the Attic Lounge, Storrs envisioned an interior furnished "...with things reminiscent of fishing, hunting, Indians, lumbering and other odds and ends native to the area."

Also upstairs was a board room for small groups with teak and Portuguese cork paneling.

Downstairs the "Sun Room" coffee shop would become a coastal favorite. Outdoors was a 20-ft. by 60 ft. heated swimming pool and putting green.

"The dining room will be elegant in a local way with deep, rich carpeting, sand castings on the wall and a wooden ceiling," John Storrs said prior to construction. With three levels and an unobstructed view of Siletz Bay, the dining room would feature a large fireplace, scultured wood panels and a portable dance floor. A gift shop on the main floor would be operated by Oswego Country Store (owned by partner Paul Hebb).

"We are striving to create an atmosphere of warmth and repose," Storrs said in describing the Lounge and coffee shop. "Our design relies in part on the element of surprise, a complete retreat from the architectural gymnastics associated with many cocktail lounges and restaurants."

Landscape architect Barbara Fealy would later describe the building process.

"Great care was taken in the locating of all structures that they should fit in with the existing terrain and yield to the great hemlocks and spruce which reign supreme in their setting giving to those who come to Salishan the experience of enchantment in Nature's grandeur."

Contributing to the initial interior design of the "resort motel" was Heinz Janders of Dohrmann Hotel Company of San Francisco, a choice made by John Storrs who nonetheless was fond of calling the interior architect an "interior desecrator". Janders, a native of Germany, designed the Japanese fishing float-design light fixtures, later trashed by corporate owners in the remodeling frenzy, and combined traditional and contemporary design throughout the Lodge.

Construction of Salishan Lodge created a stir in Oregon as well as nationwide. While the spit development, despite a variety of innovations, was viewed as a "housing development" and kept mostly from public view by the front entry gate, the Lodge was wide open to passers by on Highway 101 as was the new golf course.

Opening day was near.

Early photograph of Salishan Lodge with 100 rooms
and outdoor pool (photographer unknown)

CHAPTER 10

Storrs and Fealy

"He's big, gruff, romantic and sensitive. He is one of the most compassionate, warm-hearted egotistical sons of bitches you could meet."

Phil Thompson
Portland architect

You can have lots of money, you can have lots of beautiful things. But your value system is the real foundation for the appreciation of beauty."

Barbara Fealy

A few more adjectives could be attached to John Storrs, the Salishan Lodge architect; bully, rude, charming, outspoken, authoritarian, avant-garde architectural maverick with opinions on just about anything and anybody.

John Whitmore Storrs Jr. was born in 1920 and raised in Connecticut, received a B.A. degree in history from Dartmouth where he set numerous swimming records and saw action in the Navy as a lieutenant, commanding a subchaser ship and serving in Africa, Borneo, Italy and France. Returning home he married Mary Whalen in 1946.

Adding to his academic credentials, Storrs received a Masters degree in architecture from Yale in 1949 and became a registered architect in Connecticut before opening his office in Portland in 1950 after hearing a lecture from noted Portland architect Pietro Belluschi. Other accounts said Storrs threw a dart at a U.S. map and Portland was the winner.

John Storrs was less than traditional in his architectural approach.

Described in an Oregonian article as among architects who pioneered the "Northwest Style," the combining of local woods, natural light and harmony with the landscape, Storrs carried that mantle proudly. With a focus on light and timber, Storrs' signature was wood.

John Storrs

"It's an understandable, romantic material," he said in 1979 in describing his passion for wood. "People like to understand buildings; they can understand wood, but they can't understand concrete or strange, manufactured materials."

Trying to stuff the 6-1, 280 pound Storrs into an architectural pigeonhole is impossible.

"John (Storrs) was always quite sure of himself, emphatic. The plans weren't always thought through. Sometimes you didn't know what you'd get," said John Gray in 2003. "But it always worked out."

"Most folks are pretty hidebound in their use of words, the food they eat, the clothes they wear, the things they make," Storrs said in a 1970 interview. "They're really restricted, I think...the point is to enlarge your horizons as much as you can."

Storrs followed his advice, enlarging his horizons later in life by becoming a chef after he retired from architecture.

John Gray's checkbook had earlier helped Storrs expand his architectural horizons in the form of Salishan Lodge.

And Storrs could always be counted on by the local media for zingers at everything from the American Institute of Architects (AIA); ("the AIA is for those who want initials behind their name. The AIA is the same as the AMA or any professional organization. The weak ones are able to talk about 'we professionals' Whenever someone joins they turn gray, become Establishment. I don't think highly of most architects' work. It's a little dandified, more cosmetic than reality. An undue amount of cliche. Not enough risk-taking"); to engineers ("most engineers have very narrow training, very narrow. They know water runs downhill") to educators ("educators should learn to communicate with architects by dropping their jargon"). Storrs dropped out the AIA in 1962 ("All architects like to dance on the head of a pin"),and was chairman of local United World Federalists.

"I've done some zinging which probably I shouldn't have done," Storrs said in 1979, "and I do have an acerbic tongue at times, and I get a little drunk and cause some damage."

Although Storrs would be primarily remembered for Salishan Lodge, his other notable buildings in Portland still draw praise including the World Forestry Center, Catlin Gabel School, Lakeridge High School, Oregon School for Art and Craft and the Portland Garden Club building.

In a 2003 Oregonian newspaper tribute to Storrs on his death, writer Randy Gragg called Storrs "...one of the stalwart regionalists who defined Oregon's most distinct phase of 20th century architecture."

Storr's first wife Mary committed suicide at the age of 46, jumping into the Willamette River from the Sellwood Bridge in downtown Portland in 1967 while on leave from a local hospital. The couple had three children.He remarried in 1968 to Dr. Frances Judy, the first woman in Oregon to train in dermatology and who would later lead the charge to change the Arlington Club from a men-only bastion, the same Arlington Club which in earlier years hosted the four partners of Salishan Properties Inc. for their initial meeting.

John and Frances Storrs would have a son, Leather, who would later operate one of Portland's trendy restaurants known as Noble Rot.

BARBARA FEALY

With an 18-year difference in age (Barbara Fealy the older), Barbara Fealy and John Storrs managed to create architectural masterpieces while, at the same time, bickering.

"It took me a long time to get him (Storrs) to accept me," Fealy said in 1979, "but I've got him in my hands now, at least temporarily. I told him, you come in here you big, fat thing, and you're bigger than anybody, and you yell at them, and they can't stand it."

Barbara Fealy also generated plenty of nicknames; Storr's "Auntie Babs" stands out. But the adjectives applied to Fealy were complimentary, praising her vision, her determination, her pioneering spirit in opening opportunities for future women landscape architects. Her most respected title may the "Grand Dame of Garden Design."

Fealy was born in Salt Lake City, Utah, in 1903 where her father had a nursery business. Graduating from the University of Illinois in 1928, Fealy married college sweetheart Morris Vorse and the couple had a son, Morris Jr.

Morris Sr. died when the youngster was only 7-months old and the newly-widowed Fealy worked at a variety of jobs in Utah and Southern California during the Depression years, eventually moving back to Utah where she met and married her second husband in 1946, William Fealy, an engineer. The couple had a daughter, Susan, and moved to Portland in 1947 where Barbara Fealy developed her landscape architecture business, one of the first women to do so. Bill Fealy died in 1971.

"She (Fealy) came up the tough way," recalled John Gray. "She did it by gumption and good design."

In honor of Fealy's death in 2001, John and Betty Gray donated $104,000 to establish the Barbara Fealy Scholarship in Landscape Architecture at the University of Oregon.

In her 65-year career Barbara Fealy was well-known in the Pacific Northwest but not nationally. It has been noted that the reason for this lack of recognition may have been Fealy's emphasis on primarily designing private gardens. Fealy never ventured into academia nor authored any books or papers on her work. Working alone she developed a loyal clientele in Portland society, using her vision to develop private gardens in the upscale areas such the West Hills or Lake Oswego.

"Although many Oregon landscape architects have done individually important work, Fealy is one of the few who can be credited with starting a movement," Randy Gragg said his newspaper article tribute to Fealy in 2001, the year she died.

That movement, quite simply, was the use of native plants and shrubs on a grand scale.

"She (Fealy) brought to light a new style...recreating the natural landscape as something more powerful," said Carol

Mayer-Reed, a Portland landscape architect. "She was way ahead of her time. She was more interested in a dialogue about a sense of place."

Zari Santner, director of Portland Parks and Recreation and a landscape architect, said Fealy's work was "understated" and that Fealy had an "incredible sense of design" with an emphasis on native vegetation. Santner and Fealy worked together on a community park in Sapporo, Japan, a Portland sister city. Santner was project manager for the park and hired Fealy as a consultant.

"She (Fealy) has been an inspiration to women architects," Santner said, noting that Fealy combined work and family in an era not known for that combination

Timberline Lodge, Oregon College of Art and Craft, Sokol Blosser and Adelsheim wineries, the World Forestry Center, Catlin Gable School ; Fealy's list of landscape portraits is lengthy, some of them in collaboration with John Storrs. But their legacies will forever be firmly linked by a resort on the Oregon coast known as Salishan Lodge.

Chapter 11

Open for Business

"We have a great feeling for Oregon and the coast, and we wanted to make Salishan Lodge appropriate to this area. We think there is a majesty and genuine quality to both the architecture and site, and we feel quite indebted to both".

Betty Gray

"Salishan...structurally interlacing architecture and landscape to blur the line between its interior spaces and the surrounding coastal forest."

**Randy Gragg
Architecture Columnist
Oregonian**

"This is a gentle place. It has always been my goal to make Salishan a refuge."

**Gwen Stone
Assistant to the general manager**

A complete inventory of original artists' works at Salishan Lodge may never be known, thanks to the corporate "housecleaning" by the new owners in 1996. A meticulous inventory maintained by Gwen Stone, assistant to the managers, apparently went into the Dumpster as the corporate owners sought to distance themselves from the "old Salishan."

A plaque noting the Lodge construction date along with acknowledgment of the contributions from Gray, Storrs and Fealy was rescued from the Lodge's lobby floor during remodeling where it too was headed for the garbage. It now greets guests at the front lobby entrance. LeRoi Setziol's carvings came close to being destroyed. A mahogany bar in the Attic Lounge was chopped into pieces, only to be rescued from the trash heap by employee Tom Brosy. Gallons of paint and other refurbishing supplies were bought outside of the state, a fact recognized by many small businesses in the Lincoln City area. A review in the May/June 1998 issue of Hospitality Design described the many "improvements" including the addition of coat hooks in each guestroom "that resemble the whales one might see while gazing at the bay from the room's patio or terrace." Perhaps nobody explained to the magazine writer; there are no whales in Siletz Bay.

Artists' works were warehoused, some damaged in the process. A glass float chandelier in the Attic Lounge was replaced with one fabricated from "naturally shed deer antlers," original etched glass was eliminated, all in the name of "updating."

AN ARTISTS' OPENING

The treatment of artists and their work by corporate owners was in marked contrast to the Lodge opening in 1965 and the excitement from the Northwest artist community. Salishan's developers gathered the largest collection of artists' works for any Oregon development.

Some called the merging of artists, the coastal environment and the vision of Salishan developers serendipity. Whatever term applied, the results generated glowing reviews for a resort credited with generating millions of dollars in tourist dollars for a depressed coastal area. The resort would become the third largest employer in Lincoln County. Even during the slow months the employees were not laid off.

In August 1965 the focus was on the artists as the Lodge prepared for opening to the public. John and Betty Gray decided the best "test run" for the new resort would be to invite the artists to spend a weekend at no charge.

As noted patrons of the arts, the Grays first became serious collectors of Northwest art after seeing a painting of old buildings near Siletz in the 1950s. Salishan Lodge would reflect the Grays' passion for art as three major architectural art commissions for the Lodge were awarded. More than 200 prints, watercolors and drawings by 35 Northwest artists were purchased as well as 6 oil paintings. It would only be the beginning. Assisting the Grays in the selection of art was Mary Storrs, wife of Salishan architect

John Storrs, and Eugene Bennett, an artist in his own right, who urged the Grays to make the selections and not leave it up to an outside party.

"I was familiar with their tastes and the work they (the Grays) had in their own home and felt confident they would do as good a job as anyone," Bennett explained in 1981.

John and Betty Gray received the state's highest arts award in 1983 presented by Gov. Victor Atiyeh, a tribute to their support of Oregon arts in a variety of ways including generous philanthropic donations to the arts.

"We have always thought of art as something that could add depth to your life," said Betty Gray in 1962. "And if it's something we really like and has meaning for us, that's the criteria for selection."

In a 1965 Oregonian newspaper review of the artists' work at Salishan, Beth Fagan said "...the result (of Salishan's art collection) is the unified kind of feeling, diverse though the works are, that one often discovers in private art collections, but rarely in art acquired for public buildings. In all work by artists in the Lodge, and it seems to be everywhere, the thread of continuity is found in statements made concerning the human spirit and concerning the varied spirit of tranquil grandeur, coloring and lyricism to be found in the Oregon country."

ORIGINAL ART EVERYWHERE

Every guest room had an original work of Northwest art while the main lodge featured wood carvings, tapestries, wall hangings and wood murals. One-artist gallery shows were a Lodge tradition. Artwork purchased in 1965 for the Lodge opening significantly appreciated in value as the artists became well-known.

Large paintings would be rotated, a plan by Betty Gray to keep the art "from being taken for granted.". Artists' shows in the upstairs Gallery Room would also be rotated. The Lodge would retain 25% from Gallery sales.

The following Northwest artists were represented at the Salishan Lodge opening in August 1965:

Eugene Bennett; Glen Alps; Frank Boyden; Louis Bunce; Josephine Cameron; Havel Chilstrom; Bill Colby; Henry Demuth;

Patty Dodd; Mary Farham; Bob Gallaher ; Bert Garner; Byron Gardner; Shirley Gillelsonn; William Givier;; Paul Gunn; Charles Heany; Robert Huck; Manuel Izquierdo; Deme Jameson; Eunice Jensen; George Johanson; Laverne Krause; Betty Laduke; Lyle Matoush;, Claude McGraw; Jack McLarty; William Midgette; Betty LaDuke; Nelson Sandgren; Jim Shull; Amanda Snyder; Gen Stanley and Charles Voorhies.

Eugene Bennett, a Jacksonville, Or. Artist, was commissioned to do several screens plus a 5x21-ft mural in the Attic Lounge.

The 14 relief panels from Leroy Setziol would represent the artist's first major commission. Setziol's carved panels would later be featured throughout Oregon. Salishan architect John Storrs first saw Setziol's work at the artist's Portland studio while seeking information on sand castings. Storrs asked about wood and Setziol's 14 relief panels became part of the Lodge dining room, a commission Setziol called the turning point of his artistic career.

"Setziol has had a profound influence in reminding us of the importance of wood in our Oregon heritage," said Oregonian columnist Gerry Frank in 2003.

Setziol, later called Oregon's "consummate woodcarver," died in November 2005 as a result of a traffic accident. He was 88 years old.

John Gray, in commenting shortly after Setziol's death, said "it (Setziol's artwork) was highly compatible with what we were doing with the building design (at Salishan Lodge), and it was a very happy choice to have him do it."

Opening day room rates for the new "motel" ranged from $19 to $40, a few dollars less in the upcoming winter season. Coffee shop and dining room rates were "comparable" to other coastal resorts; $3.50 for a broiled half-chicken, $3.95 for salmon, $5.95 for prime rib.

The outdoor pool was open.

FINE ART OF INNKEEPING

Although not often mentioned with the original design team, Alex Murphy played a key role in much of the Lodge's early development and success. Murphy, named Salishan Lodge's first manager, had nearly 30 years of hotel and motel experience prior to accepting the Salishan assignment, something he called "divine providence" in describing his first meetings with John Gray and nearly two weeks of discussions and interviews before Gray selected him for the prestigious post. Murphy had nearly given up the idea of living in Oregon when he met Gray. Murphy was the perfect choice for Salishan. Urbane and dedicated to the hotel guest, Murphy and Gray were matched perfectly.

"I was very fortunate in being part of the planning committee for Salishan almost from the time it was the first spark of an idea in John Gray's head," Murphy said in 1966. "It was an interesting experience. One of us would come up with an idea which sounded pretty good. But then, after we slept on it, another would shoot down the idea. No one's ideas were given any more weight than any others and the success of the system is obvious."

A newspaper columnist called Murphy "...quiet, courteous to guests..., a man totally in love with his job." It was an opinion shared by employees.

Murphy was born Sept. 12, 1917, in the Panama Canal Zone and was raised in Sarasota, Fla. During World War II, he served in the U.S. Navy in Okinawa, Japan. Afterward, he returned to Florida where he managed several hotels before moving to Bend in 1959 and was president of the Oregon Hotel Motel Association in 1970. In 1954, he married Kathleen Kay Mainwaring.

Beginning as a hotel baggage boy at age 16, Murphy rose up the ranks, coming to Salishan Lodge from managing the 1,400 room Palm Beach Towers in West Palm Beach, Florida and the Mt. Ashland ski area.

"Nothing, but nothing, escapes this man," said Kenneth Rexroth in the San Francisco Examiner/Chronicle in 1966. "Yet, he is quiet, courteous to guests and help alike, a man utterly in love with his job and a perfect host."

Murphy was the true hotel manager, mingling with guests at check-out time or keeping a card file in pre-computer database days with customers' names. It was not unusual for Murphy to greet a guest by name, asking about a family member, according to Gwen Stone, executive assistant at the Lodge for 17 years.

Stone said Murphy believed in the "fine art of innkeeping," perhaps at the cost of not paying as much attention as necessary to financial details. But John Gray also never pushed for revenues, Stone said.

"In his own quiet way he (Gray) probably hoped the Lodge would make money," Stone said, but Gray never came to staff meetings demanding cost cutting or increased revenues.

"If John Gray had been looking at return on investment I am sure the place would have never been built," Murphy said in 1970.

Former controller and resident manager Bob Eaton also remembers Alex Murphy.

"He (Murphy) was a classy hotelier," Eaton said. "He was out of the old school. To this day I admire him very much." Eaton would later serve as general manager at The Inn at Spanish Head in Lincoln City for 13 years.

Murphy would retire in 1981 after 16 years at Salishan Lodge and served in a consultant role for other Oregon hotels including The Heathman in Portland. He died in 2001. His wife, Kay Murphy, died in 2004.

THE BOOM YEARS

In the first year of operation the Lodge exceeded revenue predictions by $325,000 and rooms on the weekend were nearly impossible to book. The unusual aspect of the revenue dollars was 60 percent came from food and beverage, 40 percent from rooms.

"This is a reversal from the usual pattern for a resort," Murphy explained. "The average person tends to 'shop around,' eating at one place one time, another place the next time, rather than dining at the resort itself."

For those choosing to dine at the resort, the food choices and accompanying 32-pound wine list in the Gourmet Room were dizzying. Franz Hermann oversaw

Oregon Gov. Tom McCall is served by Phil Devito at the Western Governors' Conference in 1973. Photo courtesy of Phil Devito.

the cooking operations as head chef followed by Franz Buck and William Jung. At one time more than 30,000 bottles of wine were stored in the wine cellars representing 1,500 different vintages. Wine sales totaled four times as much in sales as liquor. Individual refrigerated wine storage units were leased and musician George Shearing took out a three-year lease. Wine tasting classes, tours of the wine cellar and intimate catered dinners in the cellar added to the Lodge's reputation long before the wine craze hit other parts of the country. Sommelier, cellarmaster, maitre d'hotel; Phil deVito, decked out in the traditional key and chain of the cellar master, had several titles and became an institution at the Lodge, winning numerous wine awards including the Gold Vine Award, the "Oscar" of the wine industry. He began work at The Lodge in 1972 after several years in Portland restaurants and served Salishan guests for

more than 20 years, tutoring along the way Tim Tuffield, Tom Brosy and Rod Ault.

It wouldn't be long before Salishan Lodge expanded as conference and individual bookings continued the upward swing. In 1966, the first full year of operation, The Lodge achieved 75% occupancy with a gross in excess of $1 million and confirmed more than 100 conventions for the upcoming year. A four-day pageant in 1966 highlighted the selection of Oregon's

The wine cellar at Salishan was built in 1982 and, at one time, featured more than 30,000 bottles with an estimated wholesale value of $500,000. Photo courtesy of Phil Devito.

representative to the Miss Universe contest.

In 1967 The Lodge added 25 additional rooms, designed by John Storrs, and connected the new building with a footbridge across the road. Known as Chieftain North, the rooms were nearly 100-square feet larger than the original Lodge accommodations and opened in the summer of 1967 with construction by George Moore & Associates of Portland at a cost of $250,000. Also, in 1967, a 10-unit employee apartment building near the Lodge, known as "House in the Trees" was completed and opened in September.

Salishan's reputation was spreading rapidly. Mobil Five-Star awards were presented to manager Alex Murphy on a regular yearly basis. AAA Five-Diamond Awards, Hospitality Magazine, Wine Spectator; the awards multiplied on the manager's wall. The golf course garnered numerous accolades from national golf magazines. John Gray had a hit on his hands. Pete Palumbis, a AAA inspector, summarized Salishan in 1990.

"The best way I can describe it (Salishan) is calm and unruffled. Things seem to go perfectly and the staff is very affable. There is just a high level of operation which is consistent from year to year."

The first three years were tight in terms of overhead versus revenue. But nobody was overly concerned.

"I told John Gray it would take me three years of his support to make it (Salishan) what it should be," Murphy said in a 1970 interview. Controller Bob Eaton remembers the financial picture and that John Gray never took any money out of the Lodge.

"He (John Gray) never put any money in either," Eaton noted. "He made it very clear to me that we were on our own. He said 'you guys better just do it right.'"

Eaton said Gray did fund additional units in later years.

Eaton described Lodge finances as mostly a "cash flow situation. We were able to reinvest the depreciation and we could operate on a zero net income by living off the depreciation."

"My first year or two there (Salishan) the winters were awful trying to pay the vendors," Eaton said in describing the financial situation. "I had them stretched out as long as I could. It was terrible."

Conference business would later account for 50 percent of the business but Alex Murphy wouldn't allow convention business in the summer, restricting the Lodge to individual bookings.

Although the Lodge was situated on the main north-south coast route (Highway 101) and was hard to miss from the highway, leisure occupancy at Salishan Lodge in the early years was by reservation at 95 percent and 90 percent of those reservations came from individuals or families. Drop-ins from the highway were rare. Sales meetings were initially not a driving force and, if there was a conference, welcome banners or other advertising were discouraged. Salishan was a destination with most of the business from a 250-mile radius, the largest percentage from Seattle. Many individuals spent their entire two-week vacation at the resort. Repeat business drove the Lodge's bottom line.

Salishan's popularity in the first few years put a strain on its facilities, especially dining. According to Murphy in the same interview in 1970, the Lodge turned away 8,700 dinner customers between June and October in previous years as outsiders discovered the cuisine of The Lodge. Food and beverage bottom lines looked good but from a customer relations standpoint it wasn't acceptable if a Lodge guest couldn't get a dinner reservation. Dining popularity prompted the building of the Cedar Tree, billed as a charcoal grill and dancing lounge. The three-level restaurant, built at a cost of $250,000, could accommodate 146 guests and featured live music. Salishan always required men to wear jackets in the dining rooms but the atmosphere remained casual.

Swimming outdoors on the Oregon Coast, even in a heated pool, is a chilly experience. In 1971 Salishan Lodge's outdoor pool was covered and a fitness center added.

The Western Governor's Conference highlighted 1973 as state governors jetted into the Salishan airport for a meeting. Ralph Nader was a featured speaker.

On the hills above Salishan Lodge, John Gray expanded the Salishan development with 166 homesites in the gated community, "Salishan Hills," and condominiums; "The Bluffs," 32 units, and "The Island," 23 units. The development would feature tennis courts, 21-acres of common area and 2.5 acres of walking trails. A 57-acre purchase by Gray south of the Siletz Bay airport would later become Sea Ridge, a manufactured housing development. Salishan Hills II would add an additional 43 lots in 1979 adjacent to Salishan Hills

Tennis experienced a dramatic popularity upswing in the United States during the 1970s and John Gray recognized the trend. Although there were outdoor courts on the spit, the Oregon Coast weather made playing outdoors less than enjoyable most of the year. The Pacific Northwest, again because of weather, led the country in the number of indoor courts. Salishan was ready. After a questionnaire to locals was published in the local newspaper seeking interest in memberships, the 20,800-square foot Salishan Tennis Club (name later changed to Salishan Tennis Center to more accurately reflect the public aspect) opened in September

1974. Estimated cost was $200,000 to $250,000 with design by Harland-Gessford & Erichson, a Portland architectural firm.

The three indoor courts featured indirect lighting, a pro shop, viewing area and office space. The 1970's colors of bright orange and blue highlighted the upstairs lounge. The pro shop, jammed with tennis clothing, did a brisk sale with trendy brands such as Head and Tail. A single outdoor court with 12-foot cedar and wire fencing was set among the tall pines. The court would be redesigned in 1995 after a windstorm damaged the fencing. Lincoln City's high school tennis teams were welcomed at the Center, often at no charge. High school teams from the Willamette Valley traveling to the Coast for a match were impressed the Taft high school team played indoors. Mostly due to Mel and Deanie Whitman who ran the pro shop and gave lessons in the early years, new tournaments were added including a senior tournament which

is still being run. Future tennis directors at the courts would include Rick Hammerquist, Mike Stone, Becky Roberts and Ed Post.

John Gray's philosophy was always public access. None of the amenities at Salishan Lodge were closed to the public. Pool and fitness passes were available, tennis club memberships were reasonably priced as were golf memberships (new owners have substantially raised all of the fees since 1996). The Lodge's restaurants and bars welcomed local business, a key element in the slow months of winter, an element corporate owners would later ignore.

Another expansion, the 24-room Chieftain South, was completed in April 1976.

Completion of the 28,000-square foot Marketplace shopping center in 1979 included a restaurant which Salishan would operate for several years. (photo above. Salishan publicity photo)

Some long-time employees have said the "glory years" of Salishan ended as Alex Murphy was eased out of management. Although the awards continued and The Lodge's occupancy rates remained high, the atmosphere changed ever so slightly when Murphy was promoted to managing director and Russ Cleveland, originally the Lodge's sales and conference manager for four years and later the assistant manager, was named president and general manager.

In describing the shift in management, John Gray made it clear the Lodge needed to move in a different direction.

"Alex (Murphy) played a key role during the time he was with us. But it is a new era," Gray said in a newspaper interview in 1981. "Management needs are different. Alex is a one-on-one person, excellent in personal relations. Russ (Cleveland) is more business oriented. In the beginning it was a team effort and Alex was essential in establishing the reputation of the lodge. Now we're into a new perspective and need different skills looking to the profit line."

Cleveland's tenure would only last until 1985. Cleveland left for a position at the Williamsburg Inn in Williamsburg, Virginia and later the Wauwinet Inn on Nantucket Island in 1988.

As Cleveland became a short-timer in 1985 the search for a new manager began. Former controller Bob Eaton, who had left Salishan after personality conflicts with Cleveland, applied for the general manager position but, according to sources, Cleveland found out about Eaton's application and called around for other candidates. John Gray looked outside of the Salishan Lodge in 1985 and found Hank Hickox, a familiar face for Gray and an experienced resort manager with impressive credentials including Kiawah Island in South Carolina. Hickox, who came directly to Salishan from Silverado, an upscale resort in the Napa Valley of California, then hired Eaton as resident manager.

A native Oregonian, Hickox had met Gray while Hickox was manager from 1976 to 1980 at Sunriver in Central Oregon, another successful development by John Gray. Gray sold his interest in the Sunriver land in 1977. Hickox had also managed resorts in Key West, Fla, and Hawaii. Hickox would expand the Salishan corporate empire, a plan which met with Gray's approval.

"(Hank Hickox) wanted to branch out and I said go-ahead," said John Gray in 1992. Gray said the expansion would give "better opportunities to attract good people if they know there are several properties. It gives a diverse base for the parent company."

Salishan Lodge Inc. would later manage the Governor Hotel in Portland for one year as well as the remodeled Salish Lodge in Washington, owned by Puget Power. In 1992 the final piece in the Salishan plan would take shape in the Columbia Gorge: Skamania Lodge.

But Salishan's financial picture in the mid-1980s wasn't as bright as previous years.

"After Hank (Hickox) and I were on board I did a financial analysis and it (the Lodge) had really come down," said Bob Eaton. Eaton presented a financial recovery plan to the entire Salishan staff and, according to him, received enthusiastic support. However, Eaton said Hickox didn't buy into the concept and problems between the two began. Eaton would leave three years later and Ian Muirden, the controller, was named resident manager, later named manager at Skamania Lodge. Pierre Alarco would be named resident manager.

The Dining Room received a $250,000 makeover in 1985 led by the interior architectural firm of Edelman Associates in Portland. New lighting, windows, maitre 'd station and a new entrance to the Cedar Tree restaurant highlighted the remodeling. In addition, a small library was added.

Along with the dining room remodel came a new chef, one who would set a standard of excellence in the kitchen for the next decade. Rob Pounding had worked with Hank Hickox at Kiawah Island in South Carolina as well as a New York restaurant before coming to Salishan. Pounding relied heavily on local products including seafood and would be responsible for dozens of awards won by the dining room.

With a new manager, more hotels to manage, a major hotel to build in the Columbia River Gorge, and popularity remaining high, Salishan Lodge moved into its 25th year.

The 1990s would see the traditional Salishan disappear.

CHAPTER 12

Salishan at 25

"Architecturally grand, sensitive to its natural, historic and scenic setting, successful beyond expectations."

Description of Skamania Lodge by Larry Hilderbrand
Associate Editor Oregonian
May 17, 1993

"Salishan Lodge is a certified five-star resort. Give yourself another star. Everyone agrees you should have it, for you're in a class by yourselves."

Oregon Gov. Tom McCall

John Gray's developments are sprinkled throughout Oregon, from Salishan on the Oregon Coast to Sunriver in Oregon's high desert to Mt. Hood RV Village in the Cascades. Most visible of Gray's developments is Johns Landing in Portland. Thousands of daily commuters zip above the development on the Marquam Bridge as they wend their way home to the suburbs. The site of the former B.P. John Furniture Company, the $35 million (1988 dollars) project, with several partners headed by Gray, was developed in the 1970s for office and shop space as well as residences.

Inside the Water Tower building at Johns Landing in the early 1990s the small offices of Salishan Inc. housed the executives including president Hank Hickox. On the Oregon Coast the mother ship, Salishan Lodge, continued with high occupancies and was under the management of resident manager Pierre Alarco. With his mastery of five languages the former bellboy had worked his way up to the prestigious resident manager position. By the Lodge's 25th anniversary in 1990, the room count was 200 rooms after the addition of 48 Chieftain and Siletz rooms in 1988.

Alarco resembled Alex Murphy in his management style although Alarco was under the thumb of general manager Hank Hickox and it wasn't always the most cordial of relationships. Impeccably dressed and constantly picking up cigarette butts he spotted around the property, Alarco treated staff and guests with courtesy and respect.

Pierre Alarco was born April 12, 1942, in Algeria, later moving to Tahiti and to Portland in 1970 where, unable to speak English, he worked as a busboy at the former Coliseum Thunderbird Hotel and served as assistant maitre'd at the former Jantzen Beach Thunderbird from 1974 to 1977. He began work in 1977 at Salishan Lodge for one year before returning to Portland. In 1981 he returned to Salishan and worked as director of sales and catering. He was named resident manager in 1991. Alarco was diagnosed with cancer in 1995 but continued to work at the Lodge until the corporate sale in 1996. The new owners immediately fired him and two other long-time employees in a move which set the tone for the future at Salishan. Alarco managed the Riverside Golf and Country Club in Portland until his death in 2002 from the cancer.

The 1990s started off on a sour note for Salishan Lodge even though 1990 was the resort's 25th anniversary. After 23 years in a row, the Lodge lost a Mobil star. Executives, including Hank Hickox, tried to spin the Mobil snub, saying publicly "the guest is first and foremost at Salishan. The ratings are second." Hickox suggested the loss of three greens on the golf course due to high humidity may have influenced the Mobil rating. Or perhaps the lack of 24-hour room service. Whatever the reasons, Hickox wasn't a happy person. He was further irritated in 1992 when the Lodge lost the fifth diamond from AAA. The Lodge would now be a four-star, four-diamond hotel.

<u>SKAMANIA LODGE</u>

But there were other projects in the wind to worry about including a lodge in the Columbia Gorge at Stevenson, Wa.

"I wasn't looking for anything else to do,"said John Gray in a 1992 interview describing his decision to go ahead with the 160-

acre Skamania Lodge and Conference Center. "I will be 73 in July."

The final hotel project for Gray was the $23.5 million lodge set in the Columbia River Gorge National Scenic Area. Skamania was a joint project of Salishan Inc. with $5 million from the U.S. Forest Service and Skamania County officials agreeing to lease the land. Approved by the Columbia Gorge Commission in 1990 after competition from Klickitat County for a site in Bingen, Wa., construction began shortly afterwards and the 195-room Skamania Lodge opened for business in May 1993. Within 45 freeway minutes of Portland the conference center was more casual than Salishan Lodge with lower room rates. John Gray expected the Lodge to attract "eco-tourists" due to the scenic setting of the resort. Instead, the corporate sale in 1996 led to more business conferences.

Salishan Lodge played a valuable role in life on the central Oregon Coast. From the free "Gift of Music" series every Christmas to hosting high school proms to providing a first-class dining experience for special occasions, the Lodge was the center of social and artistic life on the coast. Movie stars such as Matthew Broderick and Helen Hunt stayed at the Lodge. Reba McEntyre was a favorite guest, Henry Fonda was a frequent visitor. Ed Asner, the gruff editor from the "Mary Tyler Moore Show," built a home in the Salishan Hills. Other visitors included Shirley MacLaine and Paul Newman. Tennis star Billie Jean King hosted a party in 1992 at the Lodge after the Lodge's tennis program won a national award from Tennis magazine.

But the Lodge staff wasn't star-struck. It was business as usual and the "stars" were left alone to enjoy the resort.

Never pretentious–better described as relaxed elegance–The Lodge was noted for service and long-term employees, hardly the norm in the service industry. Many of them had started with the Lodge, others noted 10, 15 or 20 years of service. Returning guests were always surprised to see familiar faces of waiters or waitresses, maids or management. Those interested in banquets would deal with Dan Doerflinger for years and find the service never varied. Guest comment cards raved about service. Employees were rewarded with trips (yearly "employee of the year" winner had a choice of any destination in the U.S.), cash and other items for outstanding service. Other benefits such as health and dental insurance, 401-K plan with a matching amount from the Lodge, vacations, and a free stay at the Lodge were given to staff, even those with as little as 20 hours per week. Management teams were treated to retreats at places such as Tu-Tu-Tun Lodge on the Rogue River. An advisory committee reviewed any employee issues. Staff Christmas parties were lavish. There were no unions.

RUMORS OF A SALE

Rumors of a sale had begun in 1995. Hank Hickox would be seen escorting groups of "suits" around the Lodge. But management denied any sale plans.

Renovation of the renowned golf course with a $2.3 million price tag in 1995 could have been setting the stage for the 1996 sale although management denied it. With Florence, Or., architect Bill Robinson leading the effort, changes at the golf course included a new irrigation system and the addition of a 18-hole putting course near the main lodge.

"Salishan always has fared well in national rankings of golf courses, partially because of excellent promotion work by the corporation," said Oregonian writer Bob Robinson (no relation to the architect). "But it never has been quite as good a golf course as its developers wanted everyone to believe." Robinson said some holes "...were too difficult for a resort clientele."

At the resort it was clear to the employees that changes were about to happen.

Main Salishan Lodge building.

CHAPTER 13

The Sale

"Salishan stands as one of the state's most enduring architectural icons."

Randy Gragg
Oregonian architectural columnist

Rumors circulated for months in 1995 and 1996; Salishan Lodge was for sale. As John and Betty Gray neared their 80s, the time appeared near for the sale. A golf course renovation added fuel to the employee rumor mill. Lodge managers continued to deny a sale was imminent.

Gray family members expressed no interest in the property. But there was plenty of outside interest in the property and John Gray was going to be as selective in his choice of buyers as he had been at Omark Industries. Managers paraded potential buyers through the Lodge on a regular basis. A representative from ERE Yarmouth contacted John Gray.

A New Owner

Dick Dusseldorp began his Sydney, Australia, construction company in 1958 with a single construction contract and a few workers. Naming his company Lend Lease, Dusseldorp would eventually oversee a company managing $52 billion in total worldwide funds including $35 billion in real estate on five continents. Dusseldorp was concerned about worker's rights, introduced employee profit sharing and was called "a man before his time" in referring to his employee relations. He died in 2000.

Lend Lease began United States operations in 1970 and made serious inroads into the United States real estate investment and management market with the purchase of The Yarmouth Group, a NewYork- based company, and added still more to the corporate portfolio with the purchase of Atlanta-based Equitable Real Estate

(ERE) for $400 million. The new subsidiary would be known briefly as ERE Yarmouth, changing the corporate name to Lend Lease Real Estate Investments in 1997.

ERE Yarmouth managed approximately $29 billion in public and union pension funds and those funds needed investing. The hunt was on. The hotel/resort financial forecasts looked favorable. Salishan Lodge and Skamania Lodge were in the cross-hairs.

Financing for hotel/resort purchases would come from a "finite fund," a fund with a limited life of seven years and numerous investors including pension funds.

Doris Parker-Grossman, based in Chicago, Ill., oversaw the Lend Lease resort operations and was the point person in the Salishan/Skamania purchase. She conducted the "due diligence" in preparation for the sale and recalls her first impression of Salishan Lodge.

"We saw a beautiful resort," she said, "but it had slipped a little bit in terms of maintenance. We were awed by the beauty and the job John Gray had done."

In addition to Salishan Lodge and Skamania Lodge, the Kapalua resort in Hawaii also attracted Lend Lease interest and would later be purchased.

In 1996 ERE Yarmouth was named Salishan Lodge buyer with a total purchase price of nearly $28 million broken down as follows; real estate, $18.4 million; intangible assets, $5.6 million; personal property, $3 million; and inventories, $902,000.

John Gray, after the sale was confirmed, had a surprise in store for Salishan's dedicated staff. At a general staff meeting shortly after the sale was announced, envelopes were distributed to all employees. Inside were checks payable to every employee with amounts determined by length of service. Some housekeepers saw checks exceeding $12,000. John Gray was not present at the meeting. It was Gray's way of doing things; understated and in the background. Taxes had already been paid on the amounts. In an accompanying letter Gray said he had seen an average profit of five to six percent on his investment at the Lodge after paying off debt service and taxes.

ERE Yarmouth also bought Skamania Lodge in the Columbia Gorge for a reported $34 million. But now the new owners needed a management company to operate the two new acquisitions in Oregon and Washington.

ERE Yarmouth immediately appointed a management firm, Dolce International, to manage both Salishan and Skamania Lodge, a move which former Lend Lease executive Doris Parker-Grossman termed a "tactical mistake," at least as far as Salishan was concerned. That mistake was underestimating from a business perspective the remote location of Salishan. Skamania, by contrast, was 45-minutes from the Portland airport via a freeway.

"They (Dolce) did an okay job at Salishan, a great job at Skamania," Parker-Grossman said.

Native New Yorker Andrew J. Dolce started his company, Dolce International, in 1981 after serving as a chief development officer for Houston Conference Services.

Acquiring his first conference property in 1985, Dolce rapidly expanded his portfolio in the United States and Europe. The company's niche was conference business as Dolce saw a conflict between the individual hotel guest's needs and those of the conference attendee.

For its entire history Salishan Lodge had served generations of families in the low-key elegance John and Betty Gray preferred. While conventions were important to the bottom line, families were the tradition and repeat individual business was the backbone. Mother's Day dinner at The Lodge was sold out. Valentines Day reservations were at a premium.

Dolce International was going to change all of that, contrary to what many business analysts, employees and community leaders told them. Salishan was going to be a conference and business center. Dolce immediately violated his company's "success formula;" "about one hour from a major international airport" was first on the Dolce list. Portland International Airport was 2-1/2 hours away (on an uneventful traffic day) and international flights were few and far between. In a later tax case, the Salishan owners would argue that the distance from the airport was a detrimental financial factor and therefore the tax assessment should be lowered. The distance hadn't changed.

Former Salishan controller Bob Eaton also questioned the Dolce plan when he heard of the sale.

"Salishan is not a national resort. It is a regional resort," Eaton said, also noting the distance to a major airport.

The roads to Salishan from Portland were (and still are) mostly two-lanes with an occasional passing lane. Winter travel could be tricky through the Coast Range, summer travel was a slow parade of RVs. Alternative transportation from the Portland airport was spotty. Even the Greyhound bus line had discontinued service on the coast.

Other criteria listed among Dolce's "success formula" wouldn't be met at Salishan; 40,000 square feet of meeting space, high-speed Internet access in each room, and "a pub game room concept in the lounge area." The Dolce cloned resort concept wasn't going to work.

Salishan managers tried to put a positive spin on the sale.

"No changes in personnel or operating philosophy are contemplated at this time," said Salishan President Hank Hickox in attempting to present the corporate united front.

"If there are changes it will be for the better," said manager Pierre Alarco.

Andrew Dolce's first move was firing Alarco as well as other long-time employees who spoke up against the conference center concept. Alarco, who had cancer and supported a wife, Patty, and two teenage daughters, had been with Salishan for 15 years. Andrew Dolce's comment when some employees expressed concern about the Alarco firing as well as other long-time employees?

"Get over it."

Hickox made out a little better. Named as Dolce's vice-president of operations and development in the western region. Hickox would only last a few months, resigning in 1997 to take a short-lived position at a newly renovated historic hotel, The Geiser Grand, in Baker City, Or., a stint managing an Eastern Oregon tribal tourism project, and later managing the posh Bandon Dunes resort on the southern Oregon coast.

It was clear Dolce's approach to employee relations was going to be a far cry from the Gray years.

THE WHEELS COME OFF

The business/conference center at Salishan was moving ahead. New ergonomic chairs, a "business center" and video training tapes for employees were on the corporate agenda. The question remained; would national convention planners, deciding between Salishan Lodge and, say, Orlando, Florida, choose the Oregon Coast with temperatures hovering in the 50s and 60s year-around, driving rain and gale winds many months of the year and the nervous drive from a major airport? Many long-time staffers couldn't understand the logic. The conferences which returned year after year to Salishan were Northwest- based; Associated Oregon Industries, Oregon Truckers and Oregon Salmon Canners, among others.

Convention attendees were always amazed the same staff took care of their needs at Salishan year after year. But Dolce and Lend Lease pushed ahead with the plan, investing a reported $4 to $8 million in renovations (final figures were never disclosed although the $4-$8 million appears inflated).

The renovations, mostly cosmetic and led by the design team of Anderson/Miller Ltd. with offices in Chicago and Birmingham, Michigan, weren't met with universal praise even though spokesmen tried to convince critics the company took its "design cues from Mother Nature and the Native American culture of the region". Randy Gragg, Oregonian newspaper architectural reviewer, said the "...gracious interior design (of Salishan) is being overpowered by the mindless, rustic "theming" of it new owners, an Australian investment firm (Lend Lease)."

Meanwhile, long-time employees were subjected to training videos on how to provide customer service despite years of customer praises in the form of letters and comment cards placed in every room. The customer comment cards, usually with glowing reviews, were immediately discontinued with the new ownership.

Within months of the purchase Dolce and Lend Lease were rapidly sinking beneath a sea of red ink at Salishan Lodge. Maintenance on the Lodge was spotty, most of it short-term cosmetics. It became obvious that Lend Lease had paid too much for the property, a fact verified by the Oregon Tax Court in May 2001. In reviewing an appeal from the Lincoln County Assessor regarding a magistrate decision which ordered the assessed value for the resort reduced, the Court noted; "However, income substantially declined," referring to the period after Lend Lease made the purchase, "and in January 1998 taxpayer replaced the management (Dolce) with a new manager operating under the Westin Hotels flag."

The Court reduced the real market value of the resort to $18 million in 1998 and to $16 million in 1999. In two years, despite investing reported millions in the ill-conceived business center plan, Dolce and Lend Lease managed to reduce the value of the property by millions.

"The fact the subject's occupancy rate declined more than the potential local competition supports (the) view **that taxpayer's (Lend Lease) management decisions drastically effected (sic) the performance of this property**," the court noted. **"The evidence seems to indicate that marketing and management practices (referring to Dolce) after taxpayer's purchase significantly affected profits."** (Emphasis by author)

"EXTRAORDINARY DISAPPOINTMENT"

Statewide, the public was beginning to notice. In his Oct. 16, 1998 column, Oregonian newspaper columnist Gerry Frank was to the point.

"Extraordinary disappointment," was Frank's lead sentence. "One of the jewels of the Oregon Coast, Salishan Lodge at Gleneden Beach, is drifting...and not for the better. Changing ownership and management have left this spectacular property without needed tender loving care. Special attractions (including the famous Sunday brunch) have been eliminated, staff morale is at an all-time low, and some of the accommodations need sprucing up. Certainly Betty and John Gray must be sad to see a project that they nurtured and made so outstanding suffer in these days of absentee ownership."

The Grays never publicly commented on the Salishan situation but privately they expressed disappointment. Gray said he heard the negative comments regarding the new ownership and also questioned the conference center idea although he considered it an "interesting concept."

Locally, Dolce also managed to upset the Chamber of Commerce by dropping Salishan's long-time membership. Public relations weren't among Dolce's strengths. Free holiday music concerts such as "The Gift of Music" for the community were dropped. The Sun Room, a popular local restaurant, was turned into a crowded gift shop. Wine inventory, long known as a Salishan feature, was drastically reduced.

Salishan's resort manager, appointed by Dolce in 1997, was John Lombardo, previously employed as manager of Saybrook Point Inn and Spa in Old Saybrook, Conn. One of Lombardo's ideas of improving the Lodge included painting pictures of tennis racquets and golf balls on the asphalt roadways to direct guests to the two facilities. The idea never materialized. Lombardo also ignored the Salishan homeowners' associations, strong political forces at Salishan. Lombardo's tenure was short-lived.

Room rates in the spring 1998 were advertised at $75, a contrast to the normal $125 to $150 rates.

The Dolce executives never understood the coastal residents' as well as other Oregonians' love for Salishan and the necessity for soothing the locals and becoming part of the community. Any mention of Salishan history was ignored by the corporate representatives. Occupancy rates plummeted. The resort was often less than 50% occupancy. New business groups didn't buy into the business conference center concept while the long-time conventions were given the brush. Long-term employees continued to leave and The Lodge began to experience the same issues faced by many tourist-related businesses elsewhere; employee turnover. Guests noticed the difference.

In 1998 Lend Lease dropped Dolce at Salishan (as it had done at the Lakeway Inn in Austin, Texas) and turned over management to Westin, a company originally founded in the Pacific Northwest, and known worldwide for upscale resorts and hotels under the Starwood banner.

Dolce and an investment partner, Donaldson, Lufkin and Jenrette (DLJ) Real Estate Capital Partners, would eventually buy Skamania Lodge from Lend Lease for $42 million and rename it Dolce Skamania Lodge. DLJ would be bought by Credit Suisse First Boston in 2000. The hotel was a more natural location for a business center (45-minutes by I-84 freeway from Portland International Airport). The company would later invest another $15 million and add 59 more rooms after the infusion of $100 million by Soros Real Estate Investments for a one-third share of Dolce. Skamania became the Washington state's largest resort.

Andrew Dolce called Skamania his company's "Pacific Northwest beachhead." Apparently the beachhead eroded. Skamaina Lodge was sold in 2005 to Lowe Enteprises for a reported $59 million. Lowes also owns Sunriver in central Oregon and is developing Suncadia Resort in Washington state.

Back at Salishan the new management company, Westin, failed to separate their other managed hotels from the uniqueness of Salishan. The company changed the name to Westin Salishan Lodge & Golf Resort. But a cookie-cutter approach wouldn't work. Formulas taught at Cornell University's Hotel Management School didn't fit The Lodge. Nationally, the Westin corporate newspaper ads with tag lines such as "Who's she sleeping with?" verged on sleazy and didn't endear the chain to locals or regional customers.

Hard-nosed corporate bean counters tried stemming the red ink. Gary Lind was hired by Westin as general manager. But it didn't work. Once again the management was totally out of touch with the coastal and state business environments. Salishan wasn't corporate, never had been. John Gray was able to reinvest whatever profits existed back into the Lodge and its staff. That hardly fit the corporate model. Phil Hutchinson, executive director of the Greater Newport Chamber of Commerce, noticed the change in Salishan following the original sale.

"From our perspective, the personality of he company (Salishan) changed a bit,"Hutchinson said in 1999. Hutchinson said "I hope it (Salishan) becomes the welcoming spot for families and individuals it had been for so many years."

Occupancy rates continued the downward spiral; from 70 percent in 1995 prior to the first sale to 48 percent in 1999. Employee turnover accelerated as benefits and hours were cut. The covered carports were empty during the week. Lodge restaurants were deserted. The Lodge, in corporate-speak, was "underperforming." Westin wasn't changing the bottom line despite heavy advertising and packages.

In the bigger corporate picture, Lend Lease was dissolving its U.S. real estate operations, selling off numerous real estate including the Lakeway Inn and Conference Center in Austin and the Kapalua resort in Hawaii. Salishan was also on the chopping block.

William Wyse, the Portland attorney who was instrumental in forming Salishan's residential plans in 1961, became the point man for the 2003 sale, trying to rally local investors to fork over $16 million to get the Lodge back in local hands. Under the plan Wyse Investment Services Company (WISCO) would purchase the Lodge and contract with Grayco Resorts LLC to manage the resort as well as the golf course and The Marketplace.

It was announced in the newspapers that the sale, complete with the hiring of an architect, was going through. The announcement was premature as investors shied away from substantial investment.

"We had to get big money," Wyse said. "We got lots of $100,000 buyers."

Asked if John Gray had any interest in buying the Lodge back, Wyse said "John helped me quite a bit (with the sale) but he said he didn't want it back." The sale fell through.

In 2003 the Lodge was again sold, this time to Spring Capital Group (NSHE Valley LLC), a Eugene, Or. company, for $13 million of which the Lodge value was $7.5 million. Spring Capital, a partnership of the Connor, Woolley and Harrison families of Eugene, also owns the Best Western at Agate Beach, Oregon, (an aesthetically ugly block of concrete with numerous corporate owners and a shaky history including a Hilton franchise), and other Best Western-affiliated motels in New Mexico as well as other Oregon real estate. The company immediately began significant renovations at the Lodge including reopening the Sun Room and adding an Internet cafe. Another meeting room replaced the former Cedar Tree dining room.

"They (the buyers) are good people," Wyse said. "We helped them."

Closing the golf course for a renovation, overseen by pro golfer and Oregonian Peter Jacobsen and his company Jacobsen Hardy Golf Course Design, the new Eugene owners did considerable face-lifting throughout the Lodge and reportedly sank millions of dollars into the year-long effort. Golf course improvements included better drainage, a perennial problem on the links, and addition of a bar and grill in the pro shop which dramatically improved the building.

The painting, repairing and replacing of aged wood has given the Lodge a fresher look.

Installation of a garage door in the tennis building allowed car shows and other activities to be scheduled on the Plexipave courts, a worry for local tennis players as The Lodge offers the only "public" indoor courts on the Coast from the Washington border to Coos Bay, more than 150 miles. The possibility of converting the tennis courts into a "convention center" has been a fear of the players for years.

Jumping on the latest craze in resort amenities, a new spa, designed by Cary Collier, was built at the site of the former Chevron station and the result is striking although some would question the location away from the main Lodge. Overlooking Siletz Bay the spa setting is spectacular–with prices to match. The company has significantly remodeled The Marketplace, an improvement from the garish colors splashed on by the previous corporate owners. Lawrence Gallery, a prestigious Pacific Northwest gallery, has returned to the shopping center. Original landscape plans from Barbara Fealy were referenced by Teufel Nursery of Portland, Or. in redoing the landscaping at the Lodge and The Marketplace. Spring Capital's partners appear to be on the right track in recapturing the original Salishan, at least as far as physical appearance of the property is concerned. The Lodge has a decidedly updated appearance while still maintaining the historic flavor.

"...as a result of a recent change in ownership, the Salishan resort has renewed style, vigor and panache," said a writer for Golf Today magazine in December 2005.

"Salishan has fallen off the radar, and we want to bring it back," said Salishan general manager Tony Pope in a 2005 interview with the Oregonian newspaper.

THE END OF AN ERA

Whether the owners can capture on that radar screen the historical sense of customer service and employee loyalty remains to be seen.

"As a hotelier, it really bothers me to see someone screw up so bad," said former Salishan resident manager Bob Eaton in referring to the Salishan's history after the Grays."You just want to get in there and shake them and tell them to do it right. Just do it right."

Perhaps the era of long-term employees and owner gratitude is history as the impersonal corporate financial statements dictate policy. From 1996 when the property was purchased from John Gray for $28 million by Lend Lease, the value dropped $15 million by the time of the 2003 sale. Lend Lease's real estate operations in the United States were also falling apart in 2003, one reason for the massive real estate sell-offs as key staff defected including Doris Parker-Grossman, the Lend Lease executive based in Chicago who headed up the Lend Lease "Lodging and Leisure Group" and chiefly responsible for overseeing Salishan Lodge operations. Pension funds under Lend Lease management decided to drop the company and Morgan Stanley acquired the Lend Lease advisory business, the core of the U.S. real estate operation. The last remaining piece of the company's U.S. real estate empire, the fund management division, was bought by Apollo Real Estate in 2004.

The Salishan name (now known as Salishan Spa and Golf Resort) is all that remains of an era when employee loyalty, caring owners and, topping the list, guest service were the chief reasons for success. The Salishan story would make an interesting case study for Harvard Business School, John Gray's alma mater; how a foreign corporation with U.S. tentacles could buy a resort on the remote, stormy Oregon coast, hire an eastern management company with no experience in Oregon, and then expect success with a business plan better suited for the Washington D.C./New York City corridor. Bring in outside design consultants who attempt to understand Native American culture in a few months, buy supplies out of state, bring in executives from the East Coast with corporate management theories which disregard the locals and long-time employees; and then expect the formula to work on the sparsely populated Oregon Coast with a strong sense of community.

Businesses come and go on the Oregon Coast with regularity. Because of its small population base, Lincoln County is one community. A successful business from the Willamette Valley may not make it on the Coast. Coastal businesses which survive are those active in the community, whether it's supporting the Little League or participating in the Gleneden Beach Fourth of July parade. The locals recognize the businesses which are an active part of the community and, in turn, support those businesses in the dreary winter months when many of the tourists have left. Companies which base profits strictly on summer crowds often fail as the less than 50,000 full-time Lincoln County residents give the business a cold shoulder in the dreary winter months.

As coastal fog blankets the Douglas Firs and the incoming tide slinks into Siletz Bay, echoes of a different time might be heard from Salishan Lodge. Honeymooners toasting each other with Salishan-logoed champagne glasses, family reunions, classical music, opera performances, live jazz in the Attic Lounge; the sounds are there but soon fade.

The Salishan Lodge shell is still there but, just as with a newly-deposited seashell on Gleneden Beach, there's no permanent life inside. There is motion, activity, the appearance of life. But the movement comes from temporary squatters soon to leave and offer the shell, worse for wear, to the next resident. A pounding Pacific surf eventually breaks the fragile shell into pieces and it disappears.

Appendix

Key Dates, Salishan Lodge

August 1964
Design concept agreed on by John Gray and John Storrs

October 1964
Alex Murphy hired as Lodge general manager

October 1964
Lodge construction began

August 1965
Lodge opened with 100 rooms

April 1966
Lincoln and Pine Room conference facilities opened

June 1967
24 Chieftain North rooms opened

September 1967
House in the Trees, 10-unit employee apartments, opened

July 1970
Cedar Tree restaurant and conference center opened

May 1971
Pool area covered, fitness room added

September 1974
Indoor tennis facility opened

April 1976
24 Chieftain South rooms opened

September 1978
Long House conference center opened

April 1982
Laundry facility built

July 1986
Built enlarged loading dock and employee cafeteria

July 1987
Built purchasing and personnel building

June 1988
48 Chieftain and Siletz rooms opened

June 1988
Traffic signal installed on Highway 101

1996
Lodge sold to Lend Lease

2003
Lodge sold to Spring Capital Group

REFERENCES

Chapter One, The Siletz

Memo from R.S Livermore to John Gray, Russ Colwell and Paul Hebb, Feb. 1963; Oregon Estuaries, June 1973, Oregon Division of State Lands; Oregonian newspaper, Jan. 17, 1963; letter from Oregon State Board of Aeronautics, Feb. 1963; letter from Oregon State Board of Aeronautics, Feb. 13, 1964; letter from Oregon State Board of Aeronautics, Feb. 1965; Seattle Times newspaper, March 22, 1990; Crisis in Oregon Estuaries, OSU Marine Advisory Program; Siletz Wetlands Review, March 1978, U.S. Corps of Engineers; Environmental Assessment, Proposed Siletz Bay Wildlife Refuge, Oct. 1990, U.S. Department of the Interior; The Climate of Oregon, 1999, Oregon State University Press; Oregon Weather Book, 1999, Oregon State University Press; 1971 Siletz River Estuary resorce Use Study, Oct. 1973, Fish Commission of Oregon; Oregonian newspaper, March 2, 2003; Estuary Management in the Pacific Northwest, Pacific Northwest Coastal Ecosystems Regional Study; Siletz Bay National Wildlife Refuge (website, U.S. Fish and Wildlife Service; News-Guard newspaper, Oc. 18, 2005; Salishan leasehoders newsetter, Feb. 1972; News-Guard newspaper, Dec. 13, 2005; News-Guard newspaper, July 25, 1968; News-Guard newspaper, Aug. 1, 1966; News-Guard newspaper, Oct. 30, 1969; News-Guard newspaper, Jan. 13, 1972; News-Guard newspaper, Jan. 3, 1974; News-Guard newspaper, Jan. 17, 1974; News-Guard newspaper, Aug. 3, 1972; Climatology of the McMinville AFSS Flight Service Area; Salishan progress report to leaseholders, Sept. 15, 1963; U.S. census, 2000; Statesman-Journal newspaper, March 8, 1991; Statesman-Journal newspaper, Feb. 21, 1993; Statesman-Journal newspaper, Feb. 16, 1992.

Chapter Two, Discovery

Columbian newspaper, Nov. 8, 2002; Local Folks and History from Salishan employee newsletter; Oregonian newspaper, April 30, 1951; interview with John Gray, Feb. 1, 2006; Salishan report, June 23, 1963.

Chapter Three, The Towns of Lincoln City

News-Guard newspaper, Dec. 20, 2005; Oregonian newspaper, April 23, 1964; Oregonian newspaper, March 27, 1970; News-Guard newspaper, July 5, 2005; Newsport News-Times, Feb. 27, 2002; The Vegas Guy, Joe Bob Briggs, August 2002; Newport News-Times newspaper, Dec. 27, 2002; Economic and Social Impact Study, Siletz Tribe; interview with John Gray, Feb. 1, 2006; Statesman-Journbal newspaper, April 18, 1995; Statesman-Journal newspaper, Nov. 16, 1994; Lincoln County Place Names (website) by M. Constance Guardino III.

Chapter Four, Buying the Land

Oregonian newspaper, Nov. 7, 1989; letter from John Gray, Jan. 1, 1964; Chronology of North Lincoln County by C.M. Andy Anderdson; Sullishak Early History (website) ;Oregonian newspaper, March 18, 1956; Indian Probate Resources (website); Oregonian newspaper, Feb. 7, 1965; interview with Donn DeBernardi, Dec. 7, 2005;

Chapter 5, John and Betty Gray

Oregonian newspaper, April 21, 2003; Catlin-Gabel school newsletter, June 1971; interview with John Gray, Dec. 5, 2005; Betty Gray memorial publication, June 25, 2003; New York Times, Nov. 28, 1984;Oregon Cutting Systems history, 2002; Oregonian newspaper, Sept. 2, 1989;American Metal Market, July 29, 1985; Outdoor Power Equipment, November 2002; Oregonian newspaper, Sept. 10, 1964; Oregon Journal, Aug. 14, 1957; Oregonian newspaper, July 10, 1987; Oregonian newspaper, Nov. 27, 1984; Oregonian newspaper, July 1, 1985; Sports Illustrated, April 28, 1989; Oregonian newspaper, Dec. 11, 1968; Oregonian newspaper, Dec. 31, 1987; Metropolis, October 1972; Oregonian newspaper, Jan. 9, 1973; Willamette Week, Dec. 1982; Ontario city profile (website); Oregon Arts Awards, Oregon State Archives; Wall Street Journal, Oct. 26, 1987; Eugene Register-Guard, November 2004; Oregonian newspaper, Jan. 28, 1968; Reed magazine, Oct. 14, 2002.

Chapter Six, Developing the Spit

Oregonian newspaper, May 12, 1993; Oregonian newspaper, Sept. 14, 1980; Newport News-Times, March 26, 1970; Salishan Longhouse, promotional material; sales summary, Salishan archives; The Salishan Community, 1972, Carolyn Hanson; Arlington Club website ; memo from John Gray, July 1961; preliminary program, Siletz Bay Beach Property, Skidmre/Owings/Merrill; memo from Dave Pugh, Decem,ber 1981; minutes, Arlington clubmeeting, Dec. 30, 1961; Salishan Beach preview,July 1962; memo from John Gray, March 10, 1982; Oregon Journal, June 30, 1962; Oregonian newspaper, June 30, 1982; letter, John Gray to William Wyse, Aug. 1, 1962; Oregon Journal, Aug. 22, 1982; letter to prospective buyers, July 12, 1962; Oregon Journal, Sept. 14, 1962; Salishan newsletter, Oct. 1, 1962; Salishan newsletter, Oct. 15, 1962; letter from John Gray, Jan. 7, 1963; Salishan report, Jan. 1, 1963; memo from Dick Livermore, Jan. 21, 1963; Salishan report, April 15, 1963; Salishan report, Oct. 15, 1963; leaseholderletter, Dec. 30, 1963; letter from John Gray, Jan. 16, 1964; Salishan progress report, March 8, 1964; Salishan leaseholders price list, December 1964; Salishan leaseholders price list, February 1965; letter from Orin Thresher, March 12, 1965; Salishan report, April 1965; Salishan report, August 1965; Oregon newspaper letter to the editor, Nov. 7, 1965; Early history, Salishan properties, July 24, 1999 ; report to leaseholders, 1964; Salishan report, April 1964; letter to leaseholders, Feb. 20, 1968; Salishan newsletter, Dec. 10, 1968; Salishan newsletter, Sept. 19, 1969; Salishan newsletter, Dec. 5, 1989; Salishan newsletter, May/June 1972; Salishan newsletter, Sept. 30, 1972; report to leaseholders, 1964; Salishan Dune House, promotional material.

Chapter Seven, Slip-Sliding Away

Oregonian newspaper, Dec. 27, 1972; Oregonian newspaper, Feb. 8, 1973; Oregonian newspaper, Feb. 9, 1973; Oregonian newspaper, Feb. 10, 1973; Oregon Journal newspaper, Feb. 7, 1973; Oregon Journal newspaper, Feb. 17, 1973; Oregonian newspaper, March 10, 1973.

Chapter Eight, Years on the Spit

Newport-News-Times newspaper, May 14, 1970; Salishan Leaseholders newslteers, March 15, 1971; Dec. 1, 1970; April 30, 1970; Salishan LeaseholdersInc.; The First Decade by Robert P. Terrill, September 18, 1980; Salishan Leasholders newsletter, April 1969; memo from John Gray, Aug. 8, 1963; Leasholder letter, Feb. 20, 1968.

Chapter 9, The Lodge Begins

Los Angeles Times newspaper, June 18, 1991; Oregonian newspaper, July 19, 1964; Oregon Journal newspaper, May 15, 1965; memo from John Gray, May 1, 1964; Daily Journal of Commerce, Winter 1966; Oregonian newspaper, April 18, 1965.

Chapter 10, Storrs and Fealy

Oregonian newspaper, Jan. 7, 2001; Oregonian newspaper, July 20, 1990; Oregonian newspaper, May 20, 1991; Oregonian newspaper, Aug. 7, 1983; University of Oregon website, Nov. 11, 2002; Barbara Fealy, University of Oregon thesis, katerine ann Supplee; interview wirth Zari Santner, Oft. 27, 2004; Oregonian newspaper, July 25, 1999; Northwest Magazine, Dec. 16, 1979; Willamette Week, Aug. 12, 1975; Oregonian newspaper, Aug. 20, 1967; Oregonian newspaper, Aus. 20, 1967; Oregonian newspaper, Feb. 9, 1991; Oregonian newspaper, Sept. 3, 2003; Oregonian newspaper, April 18, 1990.

Chapter 11, Open for Business

Oregonian newspaper, April 25, 1988; Oregon Journal newspaper, Dec. 30, 1971; Eugene Register-Guard newspaper, Aug. 19, 1990; Oregonian newspaper, Dec. 12, 1990; Oregonian newspaper, Sept. 23; Business Journal, Portland, Aug. 26, 2002; Oregonian newspaper, Nov. 1, 1987

Chapter 12, Salishan at 25

Eugene Register-Guard, Aug. 19, 1990; interview with Phil Devito

Chapter 13, The Sale

Dolce International website, 2003; telephone interview, Doris Parker-Grossman, Dec. 28, 2005; National Real Estate Investor, May 29, 2003; Jones Lang La Salle Hotels website, Feb. 7, 2001; National Real Estate Investor, Sept. 1, 1998; Pensions and Investments, April 2003; Real Estate Alert, March 17, 2004; Boston Globe, April 30, 2000; Travel Weekly, April 12, 2004; Eugene Register-Guard newspaper, March 11, 2003; Oregonian newspaper, Feb. 23, 2001; PR Newswire, May 20, 2004; Seattle Post-Intelligencer newspaper, June 17, 2004; Oregonian n ewspaper, June 15, 2005; Oregonian newspaper, March 10, 1997; Hartford Courant newspaper, Sept. 2, 1998; Newport News-Times newspaper, Nov. 14, 2001; Newport News-Times newspaper, Oct. 3, 2002; Oregonian newspaper, Oct. 2, 2002; Hospitality Design, May/June 1998; Newport News-Times newspaper, April 26, 1996; Newport News-Times newspaper, Nov. 15, 2002; Oregon Tax Court TC #4509; Washington Post newspaper, Dec. 29, 2003; interview with William Wyse;

Bibliography

Environmental Geology of Lincoln County, Oregon, Sept. 1973, Oregon Department of Geology and Minreral Resources; Bayocean: The Oregon Town That Fell Into the Sea, 1989, Bert and Margie Webber, Webb Research Group; The Climate of Oregon, 1999, George Taylor/Chris Hannan, Oregon State University Press; Oregon Weather Book, 1999, George Taylor/Raymond R. Hatton, Oregon State University Press; Maimed by the Sea, 1983, Bert and Margie Webber, Webb Research Group; Indians of Western Oregon: This Land was Theirs, 1977, Stephen Doww Beckham, Arago Books; What Happened at

Bayoceam; Is Salishan Next?, 1973, Bert Webber, YeGalleon Press; The Rogue River War and Its Aftermath: 1850-1980, 1997, E.A. Swartz, University of Oklahoma Press; This Land Around Us, 1969, Ellis Lucia, Doubleday; Experiences in a Promised Land, 1986 North Lincoln Pioneer and Historical Association; Pioneer History of North Lincoln County, Oregon, 1951, North Lincoln Pioneer and Historical Association; The Siletz Indian Reservation, 1973, William Eugene Kent, Masters thesis, Portland State University; Siletz: Surival for an Artifact, 1976, Leone Lestson Kasner, Itemizer-Observer, Dallas, Oregon; Oregon There and Back in 1877, 1976, Wallis Nash, Oregon State University Press; Native Peoples of the Northwest, 2000, Jan Halladay and Gail Chehak, Sasquatch Books; First Oregonians, 1991, Oregon Council for the Humanities; Western Oregon, Portrait of the Land and Its Peoplel 1987, Marnie McPhee, American Geographic Publishing; Pacific Northwest Coast-Living with the Shores of Oregon and Washington, 1997, Paul D. Komar, Binford and Mort Publishing; Gray and Columbia's River, 1992, Joean K. Fransen, Oregon Historical Society; Pioneer Trails of the Oregon Coast, 1971, Samuel N. Dicken, Oregon Historical Society; Lincoln County Lore, 1980, Lincoln County Historical Society; Yaquina Bay 1778-1978, 1979, Lincoln County Historical Society; Geology of Oregon, 1964, Elizabeth and William Orr, Kendall/Hunt Publishing Co.; Dictionary of Oregon History, 1956, Edited by Howard McKinley Corning, Binford and Mort Publishing; A Guide yo Indian Trails of the Pacific Northwest, 1986, Robert Ruby and John A. Brown, University of Oklahoma Press; Taft: The Transformation of a Waterfront to a Resort Town, Steve M. Wyatt; Oregon's Salty Coast, 1978, Jim Gibbs, Oregon Historical Press; An Arrow in the Earth, 1981, Robert Ruby and John A. Brown, University of Oklahoma Press; The Pacific Northwest-An Interpretive History, 1989, Carlos Arnaldo Schwantes, University of Nebraska Press; Oregon's Promise-An Interpretive History, 2003, David Peterson del Mar, Superior Publishing Co.; Oregon Geography, 1973, Samuel N. Dicken, Sea Grant College Program, Oregon State University; Oregon's Estuaries, 1974, Sea Grant College Program, Oregon State University; Oregon: Wet, High and Dry, 1981, John O. Hart and Daniel M. Johnson, The Hapi Press; Grasping Wastrels vs. Beaches Forever Inc, 2003, Matt Love, Nestucca Spit Press; Pictorial History of Otter Rock, Oregon, 1996, Lincoln County Historical Society; Little Whale Cove and Surrounding Coastal Headlands, 1979, Arness Halvorson; The Park Builders-A History of State Parks in the Pacific Northwest, 1988, Thomas R. Cox, University of Washington Press; Oregon State Parks, 1965, Chester H. Armstrong; Bayfront Book, 1999, Steve Wyatt, Lincoln County Historical Society.